HISTORY OF EDUCATIONAL RESEARCH

HISTORY OF EDUCATIONAL RESEARCH

Edited by

S.R. SHARMA

ANMOL PUBLICATIONS PVT. LTD.
NEW DELHI - 110 002 (INDIA)

ANMOL PUBLICATIONS PVT. LTD.
4374/4B, Ansari Road, Daryaganj
New Delhi - 110 002
Ph.: 23261597, 23278000
Visit us at: www.anmolpublications.com

History of Educational Research

ISBN 81-7041-933-6

PRINTED IN INDIA

Published by J.L. Kumar for Anmol Publications Pvt. Ltd., New Delhi - 110 002 and Printed at Tarun Offset Press, Delhi.

Preface

It has been said that the development of educational research has gone through three historical phases. The first phase was characterised by speculative approach where in the individual was presumed to be able rationally to integrate, synthesise, and interpret various facets of information and knowledge. Some thought that the primary purpose of educational research was to give services to the people in the field. A key characterisitics seems to be that any researcher can replicate and thereby test out the statements made by any other researchers.

This book traces the development of educational research in historical perspectives.

The editor gratefully acknowledges the American sources used in this book.

Editor

Contents

1

Introduction

Why should teachers be interested in research, and perhaps do some themselves ? It is easy to imagine a teacher thinking something like this : "We have a job to do—teaching : let us get on with it. Isn't research just academic ? Even if it leads to any conclusions of importance, they may not be published ; and even if they are published, perhaps no-one will act on them. Even if research is worth while shouldn't teachers leave it to other people who are more able or more willing to do it ?"

It is not difficult to show that resarch in education is worth while. It has real practical issues to deal with, not merely academic ones. Education is one of the major enterprises of our society as of any sociey. In mere point of size it is a major enterprise. We have five million children at school and a quarter of a million teachers teaching them, besides the administrators who run the system, the universities and colleges which train the teachers, and the parent who produce the childern. No one is unaffected by education. Under the provisions of the Education Act, 1944, everyone is to be directly affected by it for the first quarter of his life-time at least, and the national and local expenditure on it is to be of the order of at least two hundred million pounds. And this enterprise is a great one not only by virtue of its size. It affects profoundly the lives and happiness of boys and girls, men and women. "Upon the education of the people of this country the fate of this country depends".

Therefore we must indeed carry on with our job of teaching ; but we must make progress, not carry on in a rut ; and the way ahead should be explored. The possibilities of advance in education are especially good just now, when the war has forced us to think more seriously of educational reconstruction and a great new Education Act has been placed on the statute book. Research contributed to bring about the Act, as the reference in the White Paper to "Our Towns" shows. It should also contribute to making the reconstruction intelligent by revealing relevant facts and principles, by testing the results of experiments and changes, by suggesting new problems and new solutions : for research is but the search for truth on which wise action may be based. As Sir Fred Clarke has suggested, no other enterprise of comparable size would be undertaken on ground so unexplored and untested. In most great undertakings, research pays for itself many times over. Comparatively little money is needed, though plenty of time, effort, intelligence and knowledge. Yet there has been little research in education in this country. It has been better organized in Scotland, in the Dominions and in the United States ; but there are now some hopeful signs in this country. A Foundation for Educational Research was established in 1942 and prepared the way for the National Foundation for Educational Research in England and Wales which has now been set up with the support of the Ministry of Education, the Local Educational Authorities, universities, teachers and other. The Minister of Education and the Local Education Authorities have been given power by the Education Act to conduct and aid research. The need has been recognized.

The doubting teacher, however, may recognize the need for research, and yet ask why teachers should take part in it. Teachers, he may feel, have neither the time nor the money nor the eequipment to do this work : should it not be left to other people ?

Certainly other people should do more research than they do. Research should be one of the main functions of the Universities. The Ministry of Education and the Local Education Authorities should vigorously exert their new powers. Associations with special interests, such as the Historical Association or the British Psychological Society, can encourage enquiry. Individual workers can do much. But research in education will not get very far without the co-operation of teachers. The teacher has a unique opportunity, for he is at the focus of the whole education system. The essence of education is the contact of the teacher's mind and the learner's mind.

The whole apparatus of Ministry of Education, Local Education Authorities, Training Colleges and the rest exists merely to facilitate that contact. In this respect, then, the teacher's opportunity is unique. And in point of fact a great many teachers have done and are doing a vast amount of research, though it may not be recognized by that name. One is reminded of the bourgeois gentleman in Moliere's play who one day discovered he had been talking prose all his life without knowing it. A good teacher is constantly experimenting. Whenever a teacher recognizes a teaching problem and tries faithfully to solve it he is researching in education ; for to research is to ask a question and to try to find an answer based on evidence.

All useful investigation starts with a problem arising in actual experience ; necessity is the mother of invention. The teacher is well placed to initiate enquiry, for he feels where the shoe pinches. Even if he does no more than ask a question, leaving it to others to find the answer, he is making a contribution. But in point of fact teachers have done more than ask questions: they have supplied answers too. It is they who, by mutual co-operation and with the help of psychologists and others, have discovered how to provide the best environment for nursery school children, who have invented apparatas and games for the teaching of reading and number, who have devised methods of regional survey for children, and developed the bold conception of the senior school. These advances are largely due to teachers who have asked intelligent questions and attempted to solve them with such help as they could get from doctors, psychologists and others, and from their own professional skill.

Most research, indeed, calls for co-operative work. Single-handed workers have made notable contributions but the bulk of the work can be done only by co-operation. Groups of teachers who are interested in similar problems can work effectively as a team. Often the whole staff of a school constitute the most effective unit for an experiment. Working with other has many advantages. It gives each member of the group a feeling of confidence he might lack if he were working alone. Discussion locates and defines problems more exactly. The sharing of knowledge and skills makes the attack on the problem more likely of success. Very often it is essential to experiment with different groups of children in varied circumstances in order to control or assess the effect of each of the conditions which are the subject of investigation. In short, co-operation multiplies the value of the contributions of each member of the group. The invitation the Foundation for Educational Research extended to teachers to take part in com ined operations has given them an opportunity which has been eagerly accepted and has set an example which teachers can follow by forming their own teams.

Teachers may be persuaded, then, that research in education is worth while and that they can take part in it. They will then want to know how they can set about it. What problems need investigating ? How can a teacher help to tackle them ? What assistance is available to the teacher ? How can he get his results published and acted upon ?

Let us start with the finding of a problem. That is not difficult if one is looking for one. Problems arise out of experience, and if we take a questioning attitude we soon find plenty. Scepticism is a valuable weapon in the teacher's armoury. It may seem paradoxical, or even in bad taste, to encourage scepticism in a profession which necessarily relies heavily on faith, idealism and enthusiasm. But the scepticism suggested is not the attitude of the staff-room cynic or the teacher disillusioned by the "stunts" which from time to time afflict his profession. It is the constructive doubting which refuses to accept an assertion as a basis for any important action merely because it seems plausible or because it is supported by authority, however eminent. Such an assertion may have to be acted on for the time being, but the properly suceptical teacher will reserve judgment on it until he has evidence of its soundness ; and the testing of statements by evidence is research. Asking questions is the beginning of research, and indeed to ask the right question in the right way is half the battle.

The right questions for research are not necessarily, or even usually, the large and comparatively intangible issues inherent in a developing system. For purposes of enquiry it is usually necessary to define quite limited objectives. All educational problems are interrelated, but they cannot all be solved at once. It is practicable to make and test hypotheses in a limited field without making hypotheses about the whole complex of problems; indeed no other procedure is practicable in research. The teacher should therefore not be put off from investigating a problem because it is limited in scope. On the contrary he is more likely to add to the sum of knowledge if his enquiry is limited. Truth is consistent, and to add to the knowledge of it by however little is to aid the solution of every educational problem.

It is useful to write down questions as they occur to one. In a lively school, problems come up for discussion in conversation or at the staff meeting or in discussion with inspectors. Other questions may be collected from teacher's conferences or courses, from discussions in the press, or from official publications. A reading of the Norwood Report, the White Paper and the Education Act, 1944 has suggested many problems, and some of these will be used here as illustrations.

In former days a course of training in teaching invariably opened with a discussion on the alternative : "Is teaching a science or an art ?" But looking back on what then passed for School Management, one is bound to confess that teaching was neither a science nor an art. It was a superstition. A ritual had to be recited and incantations offered if the magical result was to be forthcoming. Thus in handwriting the pen had to be held lightly between the forefinger and the thumb, with the forefinger slightly bent ; it had to pass between the second and third knuckles of the first finger and to point over the right shoulder ; the wrist was to rest flatly on the paper and the copy-book to lie parallel to the edge of the desk. Immediately after reciting this ritual, the teacher, to make up the attendances of his class, sat down, tilted the register till it made a decided angle with the edge of his desk, turned his hand over till it rested on its side, and pointed the top of his pen towards the window. Ritual and practice here conflicted ; one procedure was taught to the pupils and another adopted by the teacher.

The best that could be said for the methods of teaching reading that were formerly recommended, is that the pupils learned to read not because of, but in spite of, the teaching. And in arithmetic, tables were chanted without the pupils having the slightest idea of their structure or significance, with the result that on the introduction of a new table some of the pupils concluded that it was a new song. Such flagrant contradictions evidently demand consideration and call for investigation.

To the question formulated at the outset of the first paragraph we can return the same answer as that said to have been given by Lord Morley on being asked if Politics was a science or an art :

"It's a dodge". Teaching was likewise simple. All errors were due to the carelessness of the pupil, and there was one infallible cure—corporal punishment. The efficiency of the teachers' methods was above being questioned. No wonder the epitaph of the old-time teacher read : "Here lies one who wasted all his own time and most of other people's".

To remove these reproaches and provide teachers with a scientific technique is the aim of Research in Education, but obstructive tactics impede the general adoption of the scientific attitude.

Experience, it is maintained, is all that is needed in teaching, and advertisements still sometimes read : "Salary according to experience." One is nevertheless tempted to retort that experience may amount only to having done the wrong thing in the wrong way for forty years. It is claimed in confirmation of experience that we learn by doing, but we may remark that it is only successful practice that makes perfect, and that progress results from analysis of, and reflection on, our procedure. Experience in teaching is likewise of less value than in other vacatio s by reason of the isolation of the teacher. In other occupations craftsmen work alongside their fellows and by imitation adopt their more efficient and economical methods. Seldom, however, does a teacher in service see another teacher teach. Once trained his certificate is endorsed with a life sentence of solitary confinement. Progress depending on experience is consequently accidental and slow, whereas research seeks to settle the question here and now ; it avails itself of experiment rather than of experience.

When teachers cannot lay claim to experience they set up as a "defence mechanism" against the acquisition of a scientific technique the Personality of the Teacher. It is a comforting conception, and frequently covers a multitude of sins. It is indefinable, and each individual can thus delude himself into assuming that he possesses it in a peculiar degree, and the way to win the cheap applause of a teachers' meeting is to assert with emphasis that it does not matter whether or not they know the subjects they are teaching or know how to teach them ; everything depends on the personality of the teacher.

Even where the personality is a desirable one, it is a unique possession; it defies analysis and cannot be transmitted. It dies with its possessor. The technique based on experiment and research is definite and uniform; the means by which a result has been attained are carefully and accurately formulated; thus by eliminating as many variable factors as possible and controlling the conditions we can always secure the same result when the same procedure is adopted. We pass through research from subjective or personal experience to objective validity and universal applicability.

The teacher may protest that he has acquired a sympathetic understanding of his pupil and has no need for the results of research. Sympathy and insight are nevertheless not diminished but enhanced by scientific knowledge. For example, few teachers have ever encountered cases of colour blindness among their pupils, yet investigation reveals that about four per cent of boys are colour blind, and serious injustice may be done to a pupil so handicapped by a teacher unaware of the defect; with all its acknowledged limitations the intelligence quotient or ratio is indispensable to the right assessment of a pupil's personality. Indeed, the complaint of the modern research worker in Education against the old-time teacher is not that he did not solve the problems of education, but that his self-complacency prevented him from seeing them.

The development of educational research has gone through three historical phases. The first phase was characterized by the speculative approach wherein the individual was presumed to be able rationally to integrate, synthesize, and interpret various facets of information and knowledge. The height of this type of approach was reached in the Greek era, as exemplified by the Aristotelian method in rational solution of problems. Unfortunately, this concept did not die two thousand years ago. We still have energetic advocates of the rational—and verbal—approach to the solution of problems.

Out of a matrix of verbalization came the group of service people who felt that the primary purpose of educational research was to give service to the "people in the field." To them, research consisted of the traditional school surveys, of testing programs, of many little administrative and investigative procedures. None of these was designed to add to educational theory or to build a body of systematic knowledge in the field of education, but rather to give immediate bits of practical information.

Evolving from these years of speculation and service, we now begin to see emerging a systematic body of tools available to the individual concerned with educational researc h.These tools are in harmony with our concept of the experimental approach, which involves control and prediction. It is through abiding by the present rules of the game that systematic knowledge can be added to the discipline of education. It is through the modern techniques of research that replications can be made and hypotheses tested. A key characteristic seems to be that any researcher can replicate and thereby test out the statements made by any other researcher. The individual who still insists upon a verbal, "thinking about" approach to the problem is no longer taken seriously. We hope, too, that most of the people concerned with educational research have outgrown the service concept. This does not mean that we need to discard "thinking" ; neither do we need to discard service activities. I am only saying that these two approaches should be placed in their proper perspective.

Inherent in the concept that educational research has arrived at some maturity is the fact that one researcher can check on the work of the other, test out (using acceptable research methodology) the hypothesis which another researcher has proposed and thereby verify or negate the first researcher's findings. Also inherent in this concept is the idea of intellectual freedom to follow one's hunches wherever they may lead, freedom from concern about the immediate practical applications in terms of service, and freedom from concern as to how one's findings will fit into the accepted philosophical thinking of one's colleagues. The real progress in educational research must come about, as in other areas of research, by allowing the individual who has a high exploratory drive, who has a high degree of curiosity, to follow his hunches wherever they may lead. This type of intellectual freedom does not come easily, especially to people in the non-academic fields of applied research.

The distinction between research and development has been made in this way : *If it works it is development, if it fails it is research.* I think that one of the greatest contributions that could be made by this symposium and the symposia to follow would be in perpetuating acceptance of the individual research who fails at the tasks he undertakes, who comes up with non-significant results and who explores to the utmost the various avenues of intellectual persuit wherever his interests and investigations take him. It seems to me that the real marks of intellectual maturity are apparent when (a) every researcher who so desires is permitted to pursue his personal interests ; (b) the recognition, at least, that all research is not applied (though it may be sooner or later) ; and (c) that it is not all successful. Indeed it may be that educational research is in reality, as are other areas of basic research, "a bark of success on a sea of failure."

INTRODUCTORY REMARKS AT OPENING OF THE SYMPOSIUM ON EDUCATIONAL RESEARCH

By Palmer O. Johnson, Chairman
University of Minnesota

Thank you, Dean Cherry, for your friendly welcome, and Dr. Banghart, for your informative introduction.

In a population which is so dependent on research, it is sad to reflect how few people perceive what it is all about. Research is an approach to a comprehension of the universe along a broad thoroughfare of organized knowledge solidly established on observation and experiment imbedded in a matrix of theory. It is a highway that is continuously being lengthened, widened, and mended.

We are fortunate in having persons gathered for this symposium with alert, able, active minds interested in a common problem. They have been brought together that they might benefit by stimulation from one another and that educational research might be fostered.

The symposium provides a focus of interest for persons with various descriptive and theoretical backgrounds. But it is recognized that all of the participants have come together because of their interest and participation in research.

The symposium itself is structured only loosely and perhaps it is just as well that it is. The creativity of a symposium is de pendent upon its participants. The background papers are here but without any contemplation that papers alone constitute a symposium.

We are deeply indebted to and appreciative of the joint sponsorship of the symposium. Phi Delta Kappa's capable governing board and executive secretary, the University of Virginia with its School of Education and Division of Educational Research, and Alpha Beta Chapter of Phi Delta Kappa are to be congratulated. It looks as if they have left nothing undone to provide a most favourable setting for the proceedings. Last but not least, we recognize the completeness of the planning in the provision of such an excellently qualified group of discussants.

I feel assured that the symposium will be what the planners have hoped it might be. Without further ado, let us get it underway. The plan of procedure seems an entirely appropriate one, consisting of the presentation of a paper to be followed by interrogations led by the discussants. The first paper is an especially fitting one, dealing as it does with "The Status and Direction of Present Day Educational Research Methodology." The speaker illustrated good research procedure, collecting at first hand his extensive data by visitation to the institutions concerned. It is now my great pleasure and privilege to call upon Dr. Nicholas Fattu of the University of Indiana.

is dependent upon its participants. The background papers are here but without any contemplation that papers alone constitute a symposium.

We are deeply indebted to and appreciative of the joint sponsorship of the symposium: Phi Delta Kappa's international governing board and executive secretary, the University of Virginia with its School of Education and Division of Educational Research, and Alpha Beta Chapter of Phi Delta Kappa are to be congratulated. It looks as if they have left nothing undone to provide a most favourable setting for the proceedings. Last but not least, we recognise the completeness of the planning in the provision of such an exceptionally qualified group of discussants.

I feel assured that the symposium will be what the planners have hoped it might be. Without further ado, let us get it underway. The plan of procedure seems an entirely appropriate one, consisting of the presentation of a paper to be followed by interrogations led by the discussants. The first paper is an especially fitting one, dealing as it does with "The Status and Direction of Present-Day Educational Research Methodology." The speaker illustrated good research procedure, collecting all [illegible] concerned. It is now my great pleasure and privilege to call upon Dr. Nicholas Fattu of the University of Indiana.

2

History of Research in Education

Although research in education is a fairly recent development, within the lifetime, indeed, of most of those engaged in it, difficulty is encountered in tracing its precise beginnings. An American publication entitled *Ten Years of Educational Research*, 1918-1927, characterises educational research before 1918 as "The Pioneer Period." Another American publication, *Organised Research in Education*, devotes a chapter to "Organised Educational Research in Other Countries" ; Mr. W.H. Winch, of the London County Council inspectorate, assisting in the preparation of the section of this chapter on the status of organised educational research in Great Britain, postulates 1888 as the year of origin of research in Britain. His statement reads :

> As early as 1888, the members of the Teachers' Guild of Great Britain and Ireland were invited to contribute to a study of mental fatigue which Sir Francis Galton was then conducting. In the minutes of the annual meeting of the Guild held at Westminster Town Hall, it was reported that the Council of the Guild expressed a belief that the circulation of such questions as Sir Francis submitted might be productive of much good and might help "teachers to obtain......influence to which they entitled and which they do not at present possess,"

After referring to the effort of the Board of Education, begun in 1896 which, had it been conceived on more generous lines, might have developed into a Bureau of Education Research, but which resulted merely in the Board's 'Special Reports,' the account of research in Britain proceeds :

> One of the professional organisations that has consistently supported progressive movements in education is the Educational Guild, which was incorporated in May, 1883, under the name, Teachers' Guild of Great Britain and Ireland. The Guild's interest in educational research assumed definite form in 1908. Then, at the suggestion of W.H. Winch - an inspector for the London County Council on leave of absence at that time for purposes of research—it created a sub-committee on Psychological Research in Schools. The title of this committee is somewhat misleading, as Mr. Winch pointed out in a letter to the writer. He said. "It should be a committee on educational research, especially in experimental pedagogy. The name was given at a time when it was thought that psychology as such could do more for education than it ever can".

We should nevertheless be inclined to assign the designation, "The Pioneer Stage" in educational investigation, to the period when Child-Study methods prevailed. This was the age of the questionnaire. The pitfalls of this procedure have been exposed by Thorndike in dealing with "The Discovery of Original Tendencies by a Census of Opinions." He points out there that the ignorance of a thousand people is no better than that of one ; truth cannot be manufactured from constant errors by getting a great number of them ; and that no research can ever attain a reliability beyond that possessed by the data with which it starts. This objection has been more recently reiterated by B. H. Bode in his 'Moderen Educaational Theories': "It has become a habit with us, when we are puzzled by a problem, to consult others who are equally puzzled or who perhpas have not reflected on the problem at all, and to evolve a solution out of our collective ignorance" ; and by R.L. Finney in his 'A Sociological Philosophy of Education : "A consensus of worthless opinions is a worthless consensus of opinion ; and there is no magic in statistics that can give it worth." In 'The Questionnaire in Education' Koos has attempted to rehabilitate the questionnaire and concludes : "Studies by questionnaire, as with studies by any other method, must be justified by two considerations. One of these is their value and the other is the possibility of a negative answer to the question : Can they be better made by any other method ?" And in support of his contention that the questionnaire still holds a place in educational investigation, he cites the opinions of two eminent workers in educational research—Symonds and Buckingham. The former concedes that the questionnaire permits the gathering of much information obtainable in no other way ; and the latter that the indiscriminate censure of the questionnaire is unjustified rightly used it is a proper and, indeed, an inevitable means of securing information.

The transition to the scientific stage of educational research is marked by three features which appeared almost simultaneously :

(1) The adoption by educational science of the technique evolved in the psychological laboratory.

(2) The application to educational data of the methods of modern statistical science.

(3) The origin and development of mental testing.

The late Professor E. Meumann, of Germany, may be credited with the first application on an extended scale to educational problems of the technique of Expeimental Psychology, and the publication of his 'Vorlesungen zur Einfuhrung in die experimentelle Padagogik und ihre psychologischen Grundlagen' in 1907, if not of the journal entitled simply 'Die experimentelle Padagogik' the first number of which was issued in 1905, may be said to initiate the new era. The effect of this tendency on educational research in this country was to restrict its prosecution to the very few who had both the training in a psychological laboratory and an acquaintance with German ; as a result it was asserted not many years ago that the number in this country possessing the necessary equipment to undertake research could be counted on the fingers of one hand, and while this may have been flattering to those who assumed that they were included in the charmed circle, it antagonised teachers and made them suspicious of results obtained by methods beyond their ken.

The application to educational data of a statistical technique originated about the same time and was likewise in part derived from psychology. Moede claims that in Herbart's thesis out of a limited number of discrete mental elements the whole mental lif could be built up in an exact fashion, was contained the mathematical deductive method. But it was the publication of Galton's *Inquiries into Human Faculty and Its Development* in 1883 that popularised the idea in this country that statistical methods could be profitably employed in social and educational surveys. H.O. Rugg, in his *Statistical Methods Applied to Education*, published in 1917, says : "Prior to fifteen years ago 'pedagogy' had made no use of the large body of statistical technique that had been put together." This made further demands on the equipment of the research worker, and while there is a tendency of late to make the statistical procedure a substitute for, instead of a servant of, research, there are application of this technique to the daily routine of the school which to those of a mathematical bent would be worth the trouble involved.

Binet's invention of the intelligence scale, the three versions of which appeared in 1905, 1908, 1911, helped to remove educational research from the domination of Experimental Psychology ; and whereas most writers on Mental Tests claim that "Binet's crowning glory is, not that he got together a medley of heterogeneous tests for the detection of the feeble-minded, but that he invented a scale," Binet's own account suggests that the feature which he regarded as of most significance was not the scale, but the standardising of the question, and it is this standardisation which entitles his work to be classed as "research."

The publication in the *Teacher College Record,* in March, 1910, of Thorndike's handwriting scale proved that educational research had completely emancipated itself from psychology, and in his British Association Address in 1912 Sir John Adams did not hesitate to declare that Education had captured Psychology.

A brief review of the recent developments in Britain may help to complete this historical survey. The London Head Teachers' Association instituted a Research Committee and published supplements to *The Head Teachers' Review* under the title *Educational Research.* The first issue appeared in February, 1920, and the supplement continues to be published at irregular intervals. The committee was established more to enlist the interest of head teachers in research, familiarise them with the results and induce them to afford facilities for the application of these results in schools, than to conduct research, although its sub-committees have directed minor researches and reported the results in *Educational Research.*

A committee for Research in Education was founded in 1922 by the British Psychological Society with a view to fostering research in education and to encouraging co-operation between psychologists and educationists. In a memorandum issued to members of this committee the "General Aims" were summarised as follows :

1. To prepare and publish *periodical summaries* and references to recent and current educational research.
2. To *formulate problems* requiring investigation, and to discover persons able and willing to assist in these.
3. To give advice to individuals or societies who undertake research, and put these in touch with specialists.
4. To initiate and organise particular investigations.
5. To obtain grants for educational research.

6. To press for the more adequate psychological training of teachers, and for recognition of the general need for educational research.

The Forum of Education in November, 1925, published an account of the committee's work up to that date under the title of "The Progress of Research," and from that article and later reports published in *The British Journal of Psychology*, it is evident that its function is mainly advisory, the committee not being able to employ investigators nor to undertake financial responsibility for investigations.

The National Union of Teachers on 3rd December, 1927, agreed in principle with the establishment of a Psychological and Educational Research Bureau, and referred the subject to its Education Committee for the consideration and formulation of schemes ; as no grant was voted, the efforts of the committee definitely to establish a bureau were frustrated. Nevertheless, the National Union, together with the Association of Education Committees, instituted a joint inquiry into "Examinations in Public Elementary Schools," a report under this title being published in 1930. Among its recommendations are proposals for the continuance of inquiries of this character, particularly into the technique of examinations, and into the question of individual school records and leaving certificates. In association with certain Local Education Authorities the National Union, through a sub-committee appointed by the Education Committee to advise it on, and accept responsibility for, the supervision of any research which the Education Committee might authorise from time to time, undertook an investigation into "Sound Films in Schools." On the recommendation of the sub-committee the National Union has also voted a sum of £ 500 for a six months' investigation to be conducted by the National Institute of Industrial Psychology into the heating, lighting, ventilation and fitting of schools ; the County of Essex has been selected as the area of this inquiry ; and a full report, it is expected, will be issued towards the end of the current year (1932).

Scotland has been more generous in its support of educational research, with the result that not only was the Scottish Council for Research in Education instituted, but it has also continued to function. The evolution of the Council is outlined in the *First Annual Report*. The Eductional Institute of Scotland, the professional organisation of all grades of teachers in Scotland, appointed in 1919 a Research in Education Committee which investigated various educational problems and published the results of some investigations. Incidentally it performed excellent service in stimulating the interest of the teachers of Scotland in educational research and in familiarising them with the methods of investigation. Although it is now virtually superseded by the Scottish Council for Research in Education, it continues in existence, but restricts itself almost exclusively to awarding prizes for essays on research topics to students attending the various Scottish training colleges.

Whatever measure of success has attended the efforts of the Scottish Council for Research in Education is due largely to its representative character, the following educational bodies participating in its management : Association of Local Education Authorities, Educational Institute of Scotland, Association of Directors of Education, National Committee for the Training of Teachers, Training Centres and Colleges, The Universities of Scotland, The Scottish Branch of the British Psychological Society and The Association of School Medical Officers for Scotland. Some of its activities are instanced in the succeeding pages, and it is already recognised as an established feature of Scottish education.

3

Studying The Past in Education

Historical research in education

Until about 1910 history of education was a popular field of inquiry and although during recent years it has been overshadowed by quantity production of educational research in other fields, studying the past in education still commands the attention of a number of persons. Investigating the past in education is a fascinating activity. To reveal a hitherto unknown origin of an idea of practice contemporarily regarded as new is as satisfying to the historical research worker as the discovery of a new organic compound to the research chemist. To show that a goal formulated for education of the present is sanctioned by centuries old concepts of educational values is both satisfying and practical. An aim or practice that is old is not necessarily worthy of continued acceptance or use, but the test of years of thought and trial cannot be ignored. Historical studies frequently contribute to the understanding of present institutions and practices. Historical findings may be as significant as those resulting from surveys and experiments. It is probable that many current absurdities in education would not be extant if the educators to blame for them had heeded the lessons of the past. Furthermore, historical research may be a source of inspiration to those engaged in educational activities.

Historical problems in the field of education

The reader who is not acquainted with the field of research can gain some idea of the problems studied and the scope of the field by noting the titles of the references in the illustrative bibliography at the end of the chapter. Although no precise classification is possible, certain types of problems may be mentioned. Some studies are restricted to a historical of a particular person or particular educational institution. A problem of this type is perhaps the simplest and the success of the investigator depends primarily upon locating sufficient authentic sources. The report is largely a statement of the facts discovered in examining the sources.

A second type of problem calls for tracing the development of education or a phase of it within a specified geographical area. If this area is large and the development varied in different sections, the investigator is likely to encounter difficulty in generalizing. It is not easy to generalize in surveys of present practices over a wide area. It is more difficult to do so in a historical study.

A third type of problem calls for tracing the origin or development of a movement. The inadequacy of available records frequently makes the determination of origins difficult and the ramifications of a movement are not easy to identify.

Historical problems in the field of education are more varied than these three types may indicate, but they are probably sufficient to suggest the eneral nature of historical research in this field. A problem of the first type does not call for extensive training. After adequate sources are located, the principal requirement is systematic and careful work. For the other types of problems, a background acquaintance with eduational history is essential. Much interpretation of data is involved and a person who does not have an adequate background is likely to make many errors. He will also be handicapped in locating sources.

The student contemplating a historical study as a thesis should be cautioned against a hasty selection of a problem. Accessibility of adequate sources is necessary. Hence, it is unwise for a student to commit himself to a problem until examination of the accessible source materials indicates with reasonable certainty that with sustained effort and painstaking work he will ultimately produce a satisfactory report. In the general discussion of the definition of research problems in Chapter II, the necessity of a cleary defined problem as a guide for collecting data was emphasized. The definition of a problem in historical research is not so essential, but it should be sufficiently limited so that intensive study of it is possible. A defined problem will aid one in locating sources and in most cases it is necessary as a guide in selecting data from sources. A well defined problem facilitates the organizeation of the report and most readers desire a definition as means of orientating their study of it.

To procedures of historical research

The four phases of educational research—defining the problem, collecting data, handling them, and interpreting the findings—appear in historical inquiry but obviously in a somewhat specialized form. In the case of problems relating to the remote past, the sources of information are frequently limited and the problem mnst be defined to fit the available data. When the sources are more ample, definition of the problem takes the from of limiting the scope of the proposed study. Frequently it is not possible to define the problem by analyzing it into a series of subordinate questions, at least not until a preliminary survey of the available sources has been made. Collecting data is a conspicuous phase of historical research and will be treated in the following pages. Handling the data is accomplished by organizing them for effective presentation. In interpreting the data it is necessary to give attention to their accuracy and validity.

The sources of historical educational research data

In historical research a distinction is made between primary and secondary sources of data. The former comprise remains or relics and written documents which have survived from the period being studied and which represent or contain first-hand information relevant to the problem of the investigation. Written documents are of many kinds. Charters, town records, court records, constitutions, records of legislation, and reports of public officers may be classified as official documents. Unofficial documents include newspapers, magazines, letters, diaries, autobiographies, and chronicles. College and university catalogs and registers, and courses of study and syllabi of other public and private schools possibly constitute semi-official sources since they lack the legal and governmental characteristics of truly documents and are more impersonal than documents correctly termed unofficial. Textbooks of the past, a very valuable source of historical educational research data, may be classified as relics. The title page and the preface may warrant classification as a document.

Secondary sources are accounts of the past written by persons who had access either directly, or indirectly, to primary or original sources. Typical secondary sources are reports of previous studies in the field of the problem and texts on the history of education. It may be contended that in order for an investigation to qualify as historical research some use must be made of primary sources. If the investigator does not collect at least a portion of his data from primary sources he cannot make an "original" contribution· Secondary sources may be useful in making evaluations of the appropriateness, validity, accuracy, and adequacy of the data secured from primary sources and in making inferences with respect to cause and effect relationships, where the data obtained from primary sources by the investigator are insufficient for this purpose.

Locating sources and copying data from them

Many of the sources in a library may be located by referring to the card catalog, but if access to the stacks is permitted, it is advantageous to examine the volumes in the sections relating to the problem. Frequently, the investigator must seek sources out side the library of his own institution. Many of the larger libraries have special ollections of historical documents and the investigator should seek information concerning those that relate to his problem. A graduate student will usually be able to secure this information through his adviser, but it may be necessary to make direct inquiry. For some problems, records may be sought in public offices and valuable source material, especially correspondence, may be located in the possession of private individuals. Sometimes valuable material may be located in second-hand bookstores and even in unexpected places. As the investigator reads the sources that he has located, he should be alert in nothing references to additional sources. The quality of historical research is conditioned by the adequacy of original sources examined and, hence, a study should not be undertaken unless it appears feasible to obtain access to adequate sources.

It copying data from sources, the procedure is that of recording a reference to the source and the items of information relevant to the problem. A technique relative to this procedure recommended by historians is that of recording each separate item of information on a separated card or sheet with a citation to its source. For convenience the sources may be numbered and the citation may be made by writing only the number of the source and the page from which the item is taken. The arrangement of the various items of information on separate cards or sheets greatly facilitates their organization. Checking all items with respect to accuracy in copying is an obviously essential procedure. In selecting the items for copying, the investigator should be guided by his problem. This is especially important in the case of problems relating to the comparatively recent past for which extensive source materials are available. The investigator should also attempt to determine the accuracy and validity of the items copied.

Organizing historical data

The organization of historical data varies with the type of problem. Sometimes a chronological organization is desirable.

In other cases the organization is about certain sub-topics. The purpose is to bring together related facts so that they may be effectively presented. This requires the formulation of some plan which should be made apparent to the reader. A mere recital of factual statements makes monotonous reading and a reader's estimate of a report is likely to be influenced by the author's organization of his material.

Determining the accuracy and validity of historical data

Dates and other factual statements found in sources may not be accurate. The techniques described in Chapter V for identifying errors of measurement are not applicable data, but the historical investigator should endeavor to determine the dependability of his sources and consequently the accuracy of the data obtained from them. As a means of accomplishing this, he should inquire concerning the author of the document, the extent to which he was competent, unbiased, and in a position to report accurately the events described, where and when the document was written, and what other investigators may have discovered concerning its dependability. When comparable sources exist, they should be consulted in this connection. A source may be examined with refence to internal consistency. Contradictory or inconsistent statements within a source are indicative of a lack of dependability.

Records, catalogs, newspapers, diaries, personal letters, and other writings of the period may usually be accepted as dependable sources, but data taken from them should be correctly labeled. For example, if the factual statements relate to legislative enactments, they should not be used uncritically as descriptive of educational practice. Legislation pertaining to education sometimes legalizes practices long current.

In other cases a law is enacted but observed to only a limited extent. This is illustrated by the Massachusetts Law of 1642. It directed officials of the towns to ascertain from time to time whether or not parents and masters of apprentices were fulfilling their educational duties. The Law of 1647 ordered the establishment of schools, indicating that the Law of 1642 was not functioning effectively. Hence, an inference from the Law of 1642 that parents and masters universally fulfilled their educational duties would be unjustified. Neither should one infer from the Law of 1647 that schools had not been established prior to 1647. Other sources indicate that a number of schools were in operation for years prior to that data.

Newspaper adverisements are an important source of data respecting the private schools of colonial days. One can be certain from these advertisements what courses were offered by the private schoolmasters. One can 'infer' the courses taught with reasonable justification, but not with certainty since the advertisements may not have stimulated enrollment in all of the courses listed. Numerous independent advertisements of a given subject, however, would appear to justify with practical certainty that the subject was taught at the times indicated by the dates of the newspapers. The schoolmasters would not have been likely to continue to advertise had there not been a demand for the courses offered.

The preceding paragraph illustrates an important principle in historical research. The occurrence of an event is established by the agreement of reports of independent and competent witnessses. The appearance of advertisements relating to a given courses in newspapers of different towns at approximately the same time would seem to establish that the course was taught at that time.

Although official records are generally considered dependable, the critical worker will be alert to detect evidence of inconsistency or error. This is especially desirable in the case of school records. Our present methods of child and financial accounting are a recent achievement, and it has been found that comparatively recent school records were, in some cases, incomplete or misleading. Reminiscences and accounts of events within the lifetime of the author, but written sometime after their occurrence, are usually less dependable than diaries or personal letters.

The author's memory is not likely to be complete and accurate, at least in regard to dates and details of events. He is also likely to interpret happenings of the past in the light of subsequent events. Official reports may involve errors. Occasionally the error may be due to intentional falsification, but more frequently the cause is inadequate information for the period covered by the report. Information concerning educational practices and conditions within a state or larger area is usually gathered by corespondence and it is difficult, even today, to secure a response of 100 per cent to an official request. Furthermore, sometimes information furnished the compiler is not accurate or complete.

When the data are generalizations found in writings of the period, it must be remembered that until comparatively recently society was highly provincial and consequently that only a very few writers possessed accurate knowledge concerning educational conditions over a large area. Even when the generalization is restricted to a limited area, it was not usually based upon systematically collected data. Furthermore, it is important to know whether the writer was influenced by any bias or prejudice.

The dependability of historical research

By being systematic and by checking the copied items, a historical investigator can insure the accuracy of the items as judged by the sources from which they were obtained, but evaluation of their historical accuracy and validity is likely to involve judgment and hence this phase must be designated as subjective. The selection of sources and of the items copied from them is also subjective. Inferences made with respect to cause and effect relationships and generalizations respecting the prevalence of a practice or an idea cannot be other than subjective. The historical research worker cannot keep himself out of his research, if we interpret such research to include more than the mere collection of data. The point to be noted, however, is that the historical investigator should seek to know his data and to make interpretation in accord with their limitations.

In other words, he should endeavor to maintain a scientific attitude.

Generalization should be made with caution. A particularly dangerous type of generalization is that a given event was the first of its kind. For example, first use of the questionnaire as a means of collecting data has been credited to Sir Francis Galton in about 1875.T here are numerous evidences, However, that this instrument was used prior to Galton's time. The cautious investigator will report that the event is the earliest of which he has record. In generalizing with respect to the prevalence of a given practice at a given time it is desirable to support the generalization by citations to numerous and well distributed occurrences of the pratice. Generalization in historical research requires, as in other types of research, all of the data or a representative sample of them. Some very misleading statements appear in current histories of education because of the hasty generalizations made by their authors on the basis of scanty and unrepresentative data.

4

History of the Problems of Research

Problems selected for research must be capable of precise formulation. The research attitude cannot be content with vague generalities, such as attributing success in teaching to the "personality" of the teacher and failure to the stupidity or laziness of the pupils. Many problems proposed for research by the initiated suffer from just such vagueness or illustrate the fallacy of many questions. The change of attitude demanded by research may be illustrated by a comparison of the general discussions on formal training, disciplinary education, or the "cultural" value of a subject, with the specific formulation of problems on transfer of training : Does the improvement resulting from the training on one definite type of material transfer to certain other types of material, or does it prejudice the acquisition of the latter ? If it does transfer, how much is transferred ? How is the transfer when it does take place, to be explained ? In this connection we may be allowed to cite the formulation of an actual problem on this subject :

> More specifically the problem was to determine whether the amount of such transfer can be increased by helping

the pupils consciously to generalise the process and formulate, from the three types taught, a general method of procedure applicable to the related types ; by rationalising the process, that is, by considering the underlying principles ; and by a combination of generalisation and rationalisation.

The following minor problems were also studied :

1. Is there a relationship between the amount of transfer and the mental ages of the pupils ?
2. Are there sex differences in transfer ?
3. Is the loss that occurs, in transfer from the specific type of example taught to the related types, a function of the dissimilarity between the types ?

The terms employed in formulating the problem must be free from ambiguity. We must define our terms with precision and employ them in such a sense that others can readily identify what we are really investigating. In a letter to *The Times* on "Scholarships for Research in Economics," Sir Josiah Stamp stated :

> A further object of the committee is to encourage similarity of method aad terminology in different branches of social sciences in the several universities, in order to secure the advantage of interchangeability and comparability in the results of research work.

The Educational Research Association of America issued some years ago a Report of its Standardisation Committee defining some of the terms employed in educational research. Thus it advises that "the term 'capacity' should be restricted so that it may cannote just one thing : namely, in born or undeveloped possibilities of behaviour. Ability should be regarded as the product of experience acting on capacity." In measurement the problem of validity is distinguished from the problem of reliability, the former dealing with what a test measures and the latter how consistently it measures. So incorporated have these measurement terms become in the terminology of research, that it is now customary in marketing tests not only to supply norms of achievement for different ages, but also to indicate the reliability co-efficient and provide an estimate of validity.

While it is incumbent on research workers to avail themselves of such definitions, it would be a misfortunate if their energies were diverted to quibbling over the logical definitions of terms.

5

Plan for the Research

Let it be assumed that the research problem is tentatively chosen. At least the research student is rather well satisfied in what corner of the field of education he is going to find his work. But the problem needs more careful definition. It needs delimitation from the complex in which it has its natural setting, and it needs definition and illumination, so that its various implications may become clear.

In the actual planning of the details of the study, this will be effected, and some progress will be made along the pathway of research toward goals set up. If things-to-be-done can be arranged in accord with the natural workings of student mind, the beginner in research will be able to proceed at normal rate and continuously without false starts or retrogression. It is though that the implied planning suggested in the agendum given in Chapter I, section 3, provides a logical catalog of relationships among the details of research activities to be engaged in and at the same time gives definite hints on a true psychological order of progress in accord with the six steps of the thinking process. These steps have been listed in Chapter I. They should guide the activities involved in laying out the plan for the research project undertaken.

I. ULTIMATE OBJECTIVE

First of all the beginner in research should pause to make

the best estimate he can of the general direction of his efforts and where he is coming out at the end of his investigation.

It will be recognized that this search for a valid final purpose is a philosophic act, as it must deal with entities of large generalized value. A far look is taken for social or economic values of wide import, located in the situation of the worker's interest. For example, in the educational finance surveys, reported in Chapter III, section 3, the school men have in view the concept, *equality of educational opportunity*, as a criterion for county school finance, and that is a hypothetical condition, a theory, universally applicable in a democracy. It is an ideal of philosophy.

Success in the early determination of the ultimate objective of the investigation is very important in economy of time, effort, and funds. One study comes to mind that was started without proper forethought on the part of the student and his adviser. For nearly a year, it seemed to be going, as it were, in a northerly direction. But about the ninth month, one of the likely side leads or buds that were constantly appearing definitely pointed northeast. And finally, when all details were thoroughly understood, the ultimate objective was seen on a direct easterly slant, and all intermediate steps had to be arranged for with that final goal in view. The result was that two years of time were used to complete the investigation instead of one. This waste of time, money, and energy was unnecessary. More careful, more skillful, and *more* use of the constructive imagination at the start on the part of both adviser and student would have cut the cost in two. They failed to *think* definitely enough at the first on the higher levels of reflection in the realm of philosophy.

To be concrete by way of illustration, it may be said that in a study in the field of the teacher-training curriculum such as that outlined in the agendum given in Chapter I, the ultimate objective may be stated as follows ;

(a) To find the relationship between the criterion for the professional preparation of teachers of primary reading (classroom activities, aims, principles, methods, measurement) and the items of preparation (actual and needed) discovered.

(b) To make a recommendation for the revision of teachers college courses for the training of teachers of primary reading.

This dual statement of aim may be criticized by saying that the actual *ultimate* aim is hinted at in paragraph (b). What is given in paragraph (a) has really to do with proximate objectives, as will be explained below. But it will be recognized that paragraph (b) itself is not a good statement of the large ideal this research worker had in view. An examination of the agendum in Chapter I will show that what she really had in mind to establish as the end and aim of her research was that there should be a close relationship, many points of identity, between the preparation of teachers of primary reading and the details of their actual duties as they work later under contract. A truly professionalized course is her criterion, her ultimate objective.

It is a natural thing for the beginner in educational research to tend to think of his research study first of all in terms of a rather definite title, worded as he thinks it will be when appearing at the head of his final report, for the title is the catch word, the slogan, for the ultimate objective which the mind naturally seeks first of all. He may say, "I intend to write on *Junior High School Reading*," for example. The mind readily attaches labels to ideas and concepts so that they may be easily handled, but these always appear after a more or less conscious process of analysis of the situation of experience. Stating the ultimate objective provides the beginning of this analysis and makes possible the first best guess about what the title of the study will be. However, it should be said that one cannot be sure of the final statement of the title until further progress is made along the pathway of research procedures planned out. New implications of the real direction of progress may change the working conception of the ultimate purpose of the investigation, and these will necessitate changes in the wording of the title.

The final statement of the title is important also because of secondary but significant reasons. For example, the research worker must remember that the title is to be typed or printed on the title page of the report and embossed on the back of the bound copies. Further, it will appear eventually in bibliographies and on library catalog cards, and the advice of a trained librarian may well be asked as to its statement. He will say that there are certain key words suggesting the content of the report that must appear in the title, that there are reasonable standards about length, the use of articles, prepositions, and so on. It will be noticed that in the research study outlined above (Chapter I, section 3) the title turns out to be *The Professional Preparation of Teachers of Reading in the Primary Grades*. This is not too long for publication nor for library purposes. It suggests in the words "preparation," "teachers," "reading," "primary" all of the implications of the ultimate objective. This is a very good title.

2. QUESTIONS AND PROBLEMS

A very valuable exercise at this point in planning the research study is to sit down and start a list of questions that occur to the research worker as he ponders on the implications of the problem he has undertaken to solve. A long list should be made. A notebook may be kept in the pocket; and new questions added day and night for a while. Possibly 100 rather definite questions will appear that it is thought the study *might* answer.

But it will be recognized that the value of this is just to put in concrete, separate form all that appears from any direction while study on the second level of the thinking process is going on. Making the list of queries will stimulate and aid this process.

A beginner in educational research attended a graduate seminar one time and read a long list such as that suggested above as a part of his report of progress. The other members of the group made strenuous objection, saying that he could possibly answer all of those questions in his investigation. "No," the dean replied, "he can't. But writing them out is a fine thing. It helps him to locate himself in the field of investigation he has chosen, and it gives him a better final judgment on the relative importance of things-to-be-done and on which things he *must* do in order to come out successfully."

Obviously, the next thing to do is to rank the questions that have been listed in the order of their cruciality and feasibility. Go through first and check those of greater importance on a two-point scale of lesser-greater. Then, examine the *greater* list and underline the five or six of most importance, always keeping the ultimate aim of the whole process in mind. Then, put in parenthesis the question *par excellence*, the key query of the entire list, the real basic thing that the study is after. Of course, there must be constant judgments on the practicability of queries finally accepted. Any should be rejected whose attempted solution does not appear to be feasible at that time with abilities and resources available.

For example, the study referred to above might appear as follows at this point, just a few of the total list of questions being given.

3. THE THESIS

Both the logical and psychological next step is to state the thesis of the study in definite, declarative sentence form. (See Chapter I, section 3, for the technical meaning of the word *thesis*.) It will be recognized that this means the next step in the thinking process, the formulation of a hypothesis, or scientific guess, appearing most likely at this point in reflective thought. It will be understood, too, that the thesis will be just the problem itself stated positively, not as a question. For example, the central thesis of the teacher-training study used for illustration here might be worded as follows :

I believe this to be true, that

THESIS

The details of the objectives for a preparatory curriculum for teachers of primary reading, the content of the courses offered, must be discovered, first of all, among the actual activities of such teachers while at work in the public school classroom,

and my investigation will uphold this statement of fact and prove it to be true. (See Chapter I, section 3, for another possible form of statement.)

Notice that this is a declaration of belief, a truth of rather large value in the judgment of the research worker, which he is prepared to defend and which he *does* defend and substantiate in the course of the prosecution of his study and its final report.

A review of this section and the two preceding will reveal to the beginner in educational research the rather close relationship which exists among the concepts, ultimate objective, title, question, problem, and thesis. They are all found on the higher levels of reflective thought, all generalizations of rather large value. It cleverly conceived and stated, the ultimate objective becomes the title and the most crucial query, then the central problem ; and, when accepted by the worker as an ideal for his research, it emerges as the thesis.

4. PROCEDURES AND TECHNICS

In progress toward the final goal set up, the ultimate objective, certain intermediate stages must be passed, as in starting to drive from Denver to Chicago, for example, one must pass through Omaha, Cedar Rapids, and so forth, on the Lincoln Highway or by way of Lincoln and Kansas City on the D.L.D. It is a problem of making out the route to be traveled from beginning to end of the research journey.

The question that the beginner in educational research should settle now is: What are the important steps, the necessary things-to-be-done, after defining my problem in terms of title, thesis, and ultimate aim ? The answers require careful consideration, the exercise of a high degree of constructive imagination, industry, perseverance, patience, and time. The suggestion is that as soon as any tentative decisions in the matter be made, they be reduced to writing at once and then be subjected to constant revision as new light appears on the details of proper procedures. In this way no progress once made will be lost. It will not be necessary to go back to the zero point every time the task appears above the conscious level of thought. It may be taken up at the stage of progress already reached and shoved ahead nearer to the final successful arrangement as a definite list of necessary research procedures.

Referring to the illustrative study above again, it will be seen that at the end of ten weeks of work the procedures more or less definitely decided on were :

(a) To read all related background literature.

(b) To make an analysis of pupil activities provided for an actual primary reading courses used in the public schools.

(c) To analyze suggestions on purposes, principles, and methods given by educational experts.

(d) To analyze the content of primary reading tests.

(e) To make an analysis of the present offerings in teacher-training curriculums for primary teachers.

(f) To get the judgment of specialists in primary reading on the best content for a teacher-training curriculum for teachers of primary reading.

(g) To classify all data gathered in accordance with good methods already tried out and evaluated for tabular and graphic representation.

(h) To discuss and interpret all material in the light of objectives set up.

(i) To arrange the final report in logical chapter sequence with pertinent section discussions.

The list of procedures gives the best guess on *what* must be done in the carrying through of the study engaged in by the research beginner. But he must decide in minute detail just *how* he plans to do each thing that must be done. He must settle on all of the technies for each item of procedure, the list of methods to be used at each step taken toward the final goal of completion, ultimate objective. And in this the worker cannot be too scrupulously careful, too industrious in cudgeling his brain about the least detail of techinc, too meticulous in writing down every last item of "*how*" which he can get pre-knowledge of. A mistake here may cost money, and certainly will cost time. A careful answer for each item of procedure must be devised and set down to the question : Just what must I do at this point to make sure and valuable the step decided upon ?

Too much space in the agendum cannot be given to these answers. The sample outline given above (Chapter I, section 3) may be justly criticized in that its "Methods" statements are too short, leave too much unsaid. But it will be remembered that this was written after only ten weeks of work. Thinking did not stop at this point of progress. If the agendum were written out again during the third quarter of work, it would include *all* necessary details.

Taking an illustration from this agendum, it will be seen that Procedure III, "Determine the aims, psychological principles, and methods which primary teachers must understand in order to teach primary reading," is followed by this statement of methods thought out :

> An analysis of expert opinion will be made, using many book and magazine articles dealing with these topics. The *Eighteenth* and the *Twenty-fourth Yearbooks* of the National Society for the Study of Education will be inclu-

ded. The entire bibliography is very long, and is not given here in complete form.

It will be seen (a) that at least a better sample (possibly a dozen items) of the bibliography to be used for informational analysis should have been given, (b) that the details of the method of analysis ought to have been explained and illustrated, (c) that necessary differences in technics used for the analyses of *aims*, *principles* and *methods* ought to have been explained, and so on. In fact, the actual details of every item of method should be given here. They will all appear finally as research activities later during the carrying out of the study, and their statement at this point will make sure that every items of *method* shall be done in logical and psychological order, and none be omitted.

5. PROXIMATE OBJECTIVES

Every item of procedure is a step toward the ultimate aim set up. It is in fact a proximate objective. It is a valuable exercise at this point in the thinking process to state all procedures in logical order and in generalized form, placing them above the ultimate objective in the agendum so that a check may be made on their value as actual steps toward the final outcome desired.

The primary teacher-training curriculum study outlined above states these proximate objectives as follows :

1. To determine what actual reading work primary grade teachers are expected to each.

2. To determine the aims, psychological principles, and methods and developments in measurement that primary teachers should undertand in order to teach primary reading effectively.

3. To determine the contribution of the content of primary reading tests to the problem of a good teacher-training course in primary reading.

4. To determine the amount and character of training that our teacher-training institutions are giving to prepare for the above needs.

5. To determine the judgment of a jury of frontier thinkers on the content of a teacher-training course in primary reading.

It will be seen that each of the procedures after the first, which deals with work reading in the field of interest, is represented until one reaches the point where material gathered is to be classified, discussed, and interpreted.

The beginner in educational research has now in concrete logical form on the first page of his agendum a complete statement of the essential parts of his research project. This is very valuable to him and to his adviser as a check on the validity of the scientific thinking process in which they are engaged. Does the statement of the ultimate objective give adequately the actual outcome sought ? Is the title the same concept in epitome ? Do the proximate objectives represent the best guess of necessary steps which must be taken in order to arrive successfully at the final goal of effort ? Affirmative answers to these questions will give the research workers confidence to invest further capital in the enterprise undertaken in the form of time, energy, and funds needed.

But a necessary caution here is that the thinking process must not cease at this point of progress. The mind must be kept receptive to new insights and further evidence, which must be permitted to change the details of proximate aims or even to modify the conception held of the real import of the ultimate objective itself, if necessary. The acceptance of hypotheses and theories is a normal activity in the process of reflective thought. But their status must always be tentative. A closed mind, blocked by prejudices or dearly held beliefs, never is able to reach the creditably high inclusive levels of the scientific thinking process.

6. CHAPTER HEADS AND SECTION TITLES

Experience and knowledge of the psychology of thinking have shown that it is a very valuable thing and strictly in accord with the way the normal mind insists upon working (Chapter I, section 3), to write down just at this point the first guess as to what the big centers of discussion will be together with whatever can be thought out for detailed topics under each. These are the chapter titles and the section topics of the final report.

If the necessary *procedures* have been carefully set down, as suggested above, and if each has been stated as a *proximate objective*, the research student will find there the best hint for the organization of a logical trend of thought in the final report of his study, the best suggestion on the content of the several chapters which must be written. It is not suggested that it is always possible actually to restate each proximate objective in title form and be sure that one has an outline of chapter heads for his report. This often occurs ; but often, too, it does not. It may be that two of the proximate aims are so closely related that their content should appear as a logical unit of discussion in a single chapter. Or, it may be that under another proximate objective, two or three vital technics of attack appear on the "Methods" side which should each be given a chapter.

This suggests a likely source of information as to the subsumed points of discussion in each chapter, the section titles. These may be looked for first of all among the parallel methods statements to the right. If these are very carefully thought out and minutely written in, one may have hints on all that needs to be said in each chapter discussion.

The chapter and section titles in the teacher-training curriculum study already referred to are given below as the appeared at the close of the tenth week of work. Notice that the section titles are very well put down except for Chapter 7 The imagination balked there.

THE PROFESSION PREPARATION OF TEACHERS OF READING IN THE PRIMARY GRADES

Chapter I. Curriculum making for Teachers of Primary Reading

1. Past Practics in Curriculum-making.
2. Activity Analysis as a Method of Curriculum-making.
3. Consulting "Frontier Thinkers".
4. The Hypothesis on Which This Study is Based.
5. Summary.

Chapter II. The Objectives of Primary Reading

1. Method of Arriving at Objectives.
2. The Final List.
3. Summary.

Chapter III. The Nature of the Reading Process

1. Characteristics of Reading
2. Eye-Movement Studies.
3. The Fixation Pause
4. The Perceptual Span
5. Types of Reading [illegible]ecilities and Difficulties.
6. Summary [illegible]acl

Chapter IV. Reading Activi[illegible]es in the Primary Grades

1. Methods of Teaching Beginning Reading.
2. Rate of Reading
3. Remedial Work
4. Summary

Chapter V. The Duties of Teachers of Primary Reading

1. Method of Analysis
2. Results of the Informational Analysis,
3. Summary

Chapter VI. Teacher-Training Offerings

1. Method of Analysis
2. Results of the Analysis
3. Summary

Chapter VII. Colorado State Teachers College Offerings

Chapter VIII. Summary, Conclusions, and Recommendations

1. General Summary
2. Conclusions
3. Recommendations
4. Further Studies Needed

Notice that the chapter heads above except the last are *distinctively* stated. They are not simply :

Chapter I. Introduction

Chapter II. Methods

Chapter III. Results

Chapter IV. Summary and Conclusions

It is true that reports of investigations organized like this may be found in the libraries. But these chapter titles suggest nothing about the *content* of the report, and that is just what they should do. They should be *distinctive*. There are always several big logical units to be found among the material resulting from the study, and these will appear as chapter heads. If the beginner's imagination cannot guess these at all so early in the research, he may get hints as to what they will be by examining reports of investigations similar to his written by other workers. These may almost always be easily found. Hardly any educational research neophyte is at work in a virgin field.

Exceptions to this point of view may occur in the titles of the first and the last chapters of the report. It is noticed that the title for Chapter VIII above is summary, conculsions. and Recommendations ; and this is very good. Likewise, successful reports often organize the first chapter.

Chapter I. Introduction

1. Previous Studies in the Field.
2. The Need for this Investigation.
3. The Problem
4. The Thesis
5. Procedures and Technics.
6. Brief Summary of Findings.

The last section above, the sixth, is very hard to write. But it is very useful. It is section 1 of Chapter VIII, for example, "Essential Content of the Study," reduced to its smallest possible bulk, possibly one paragraph. The writing of these two sections, certainly a section like section 1 in the last chapter, which is the big, detaied summary of the entire study, is an obligation on the part of the research worker. He must put all of the details (background, methods, results, conclusions, and so on) somewhere in condensed form so that the busy student of education may be able to get it with the least expenditure of time. The last chapter is the logical place for this, unless one uses an entire *first* chapter for this purpose, as is done in many survey reports which are written, for example, to get over a series of recommendations to a legislature.

Comment should be made also on the last suggested section of the last chapter, "Further Research Needed." The research worker should begin to keep notes for the writing of this section as soon as he begins his planning. If his mind works with fertility, many side problems will be constantly budding out of the main stem of thought growth. These are suggestions for other related studies that ought to be undertaken if a complete, inclusive investigation is to be carried through in the filed of endeavour. All of these that cannot be made by the research worker himself at this time must be carefully listed and briefly discussed in the last section of his report. This is a test of his grasp of the whole question, and it insures continuity in research by telling the next student what next things should be done. Note that Kelly in his Commonwealth

Fund study gives these suggestions on important related researches that should be made throughout his entire report, listing them after each important unit of discussion instead of grouping them all under a single heading at the close of his book.

7. SUMMARY

In planning the actual carrying out of the details of the investigation decided on by the beginner in educational research and his adviser, care should be taken that things-to-be-done are in a probable psychological order. Experience has shown that the discovery of the final objective is the first matter for consideration and that this when found will suggest a valid title, which should be worded in proper form for bibliography and library purposes. In attempting to locate the central problem involved in the proposed research project, all queries arising in its consideration should be set down for evaluation and ranking, and the most crucial question restated in both problem and thesis form. Then, it is logical to decide on the successive steps to be taken in progress toward the goal sought, as well as on the details of technics to be employed in each procedure. Finally, the entire process of thought will be clarified and its related parts made more definite if the large foci of discussion and interpretation are outlined, the chapter and section titles for the final report.

8. RESEARCH EXERCISES

A. Analyze a master's report in terms of (a) ultimate objective, (b) title, (c) problem, (d) thesis, (e) procedures, each with its (f) methods, (g) proximate objectives.

B. Analyze a doctor's dissertation in the same way.

C. Analyze a research made in some field other than the social sciences in the same way. For example, take one found in the Engineering Foundation narratives, in *The Microbe Hunters*, in Pasteur's biography.

D. Make a score card for the evaluation of an investigation in the field of educational research, using for the main items of the scale the points of discussion in the above section and including also the bibliography treated in Chapter V.

E. Interview an educator who has a master's degree and make a list of the items of his experience in making the research study offered in partial fulfillment of the requirements for the degree.

F. Interview a doctor of philosophy in the same manner.

G. Analyze five reports of masters' studies and judge them as to whether the chapter and section titles are arranged both logically and psychologically.

H. Analyze five doctor's studies in the same manner.

I. Get definitely stated criteria for a good title for an educational research report from the head librarian and analyze five titles of reports found in the educational journals, five book titles, and five titles of masters' reports.

J. Organize an agendum for a study suggested by one of these topics :

(a) The distribution of state school funds in the state of your residence.

(b) The relationsh between scholarship and the amount of money spent per capita.

(c) A comparison of the relation value of extensive and intensive procedure in teaching literature.

(d) A study of the elements that produce success in arithmetic.

(e) The relative efficiency of comprehension and reten tion of information presented in fact and story form.

(f) The growth of Dutch Colonial schools in New York.

(g) The preparation of teachers of high-school English.

(h) The relative difficulty of arithmetical combinations.

(i) Contribution of Germans to our public education.

(j) Determination of factors that tend to eliminate high-school pupils.

K. What research problems to you see in these situations? Organize each research study found in terms of title, objectives, and procedures with technics to be used.

(a) You are superintendent of schools in a small city like Longmont, Colorado. A number of your patrons believe that the secondary-school curriculum should be extended for two years beyond the twelfth grade and organized as a local junior college. They have interested the chamber of commerce to request the board of education to do this. The chamber of commerce has heard that Trinidad has a junior college. The board of education asks you for a report and recommendations in the matter.

(b) You are an elementary-school supervisor in a city system of about 7,000 pupils. The superintendent of schools has just returned from a national meeting where he has heard a number of addresses on pre-school education. He asks you what it is all about and what you recommend for the local system.

(c) You are director of research in a school system in a city of about 300,000 population. You have reported to the superintendent a pupil unit cost in the elementary schools that is much higher than that in ten other cities of about the same size. He asks you to make a study of class size in the elementary schools. He wishes to know whether he may lower pupils unit costs by increasing class enrollment, and without lowering the efficiency of public education in the local system.

(d) You are a bioliogy teacher in a teachers college. You make certain definite daily reading assignments to your freshman class, but the majority of the students come back day after day knowing very little about what they have read, and in the final test their residuum of information is meager indeed.

(e) You are a young master-of-arts graduate from a teachers college just elected to the principalship of a junior-high school of 350 pupils. Your new superintendent asks your judgment on the desirability of changing the daily program of the high school to have lengthened periods (80 minutes) instead of 45-minute periods as at present.

6

The Design of Educational Research

OSCAR KEMPTHORNE
Professor of Statistics
Statistical Laboratory
Iowa State University

Introduction

Research in education appears to revolve around two basic activities :

(1) the description of the past and present situation with regard to methods and results ;

(2) the exploration of input-output relationships.

The role of description is simply to know what the facts are, and the tool is survey design and analysis. Some of these facts will not be liked and the question then arises of what should be done to bring the situation to a status which is liked. This is the problem of input-output relationships. For example, on some basis it is decided that students do not use the English language properly and possible ways of bringing about proper use of language, such as taking a Latin course for two years, are suggested. These are man-controlled inputs. If two years of Latin can be shown to improve use of language without having other deleterious effects, then the appropriate individuals would rule that students should have two years of Latin.

There are essentially two distinct procedures of studying input-output relationships :

(1) the analytical survey and

(2) the designed experiment.

In the analytical survey one is essentially looking for two "individuals" which have been subjected entirely to the same variants of all forces but one. With regard to the exceptional force one individual has been exposed to one variant and the other to another variant, as, for example, one studied Latin for two years while the other studied French ; but in all other respects the two individuals had identical abilities and environment. Whatever difference arises one attributes to the different effect of one variant to the other variant. Studies of separated identical twins fall into this category, the hope being that the identity of genotype will lead to no difference except that due to difference in environment. School systems are compared in this way One will try to find, for example, two school systems in which the cultural and ethnological background, level of income, and so on are the same ; but one of the systems does not allow high school students to drive automobiles to school and the other does.

This is, of course, the most primitive situation. The models we fit do not generally have such simplicity. One may fit a multiple classification model, in which no two such individuals occur but in which effects may be inferred in some stepwise manner. To understand what is meant, consider the following illustrative data :

"Treatment"	Mean
$a_0\ b_0\ c_0$	10

$a_0\ b_1\ c_1$	12
$a_1\ b_0\ c_1$	16
$a_1\ b_1\ c_0$	14

If we assume no interaction, so that the change from a_0 to a_1; from b_0 to b_1; and from c_0 to c_1 produce changes A, B, and C respectively :

$$A+C=2$$

$$A+C=6$$

$$A+B=4$$

So A=4, B=0, C=2. We are therefore able to guess the effects of the three factors, if we can provide the assumption of no interaction. In the same sort of way one may postulate any sort of model which contains effects of presumed variants in forces to which individuals have been subjected. The difficulties of drawing reliable and convincing conclusions in this situation are well known but should not deter us, because the great bulk of data that will be available to us will be of this type. In the designed experiment to experimenter chooses his experimental material and milieu and imposes variations in the way experimental material is handled, *i.e.*, imposes different treatments to different parts of the experimental material. Since the choice of treatment for any part of the experimental material is done by the experimenter, whatever differences are found are properly attributed to the effects of the treatments.

I think it is essential to emphasize that in essentially all scientific activities we are concerned with experimental conclusions. To illustrate, a nonexperimental conclusion that seems by all accounts to be substantiated beyond doubt is that the incidence of lung cancer for smokers is greater than for nonsmokers. This is an observational or historical fact. As a fact, it could be useful, for example, in suggesting that since lung cancer is sometimes (somewhat at least) curable, smokers should have periodic X-ray lung examinations, Even in this use, however, we have to depend, for justification, on the assumption that individuals arise from some sort of stationary random process, because the fact of history may not turn out to be a fact for the future.

However, the smoking—lung cancer issue raises a more serious and relevant question : Should smokers be persuaded to give up smoking and should we endeavor to prevent our young people from smoking ? To answer these questions we need an experimental-type conclusion that the effect of preventing or dissuading individuals who want to smoke from doing so will reduce the probability of their getting lung cancer and will not alter other attributes sufficiently to outweight this gain.

The existence of the association of smoking and lung cancer is only slight evidence for the efficacy of terminating smoking. Of course, if this is the only evidence available we may, as individuals, decide to take account of it on the basis that it is possibly indicative of a causal effect and we want to hedge. It might be observed, for instance, that Harvard graduates make higher incomes ten years after graduation than graduates at the University of Minnesota. The immediate reaction of the ordinary parent is to make every attempt to get his son into Harvard. But everyone who gives a little thought to the question realizes that this experimental-type conclusion is quite fallacious. One can only hope that one of these days our popular and semipopular press will realize that superficially obtained inferences of this type are usually erroneous. I believe it is very dangerous to attach any name such as *ex post facto* experiment to an analytical survey.

In this paper I shall be concerned with the drawing of experimental-type or causal inferences when the research worker has control over the inputs or stimuli and the experimental situation.

The Two Fundamental Problems of Experimental Inference

In my view, the fundamental difficulties of inferring the possible effects of man-controlled inputs are two :

1. In any comparison of the effects of, say, two different imposed inputs, we can never obtain two *identical* individuals to which one of the inputs can be applied and to the other of which the other input can be applied.
2. We are always concerned with individuals and situations other than those on which we can make experimental comparisons.

Both of these seem to me to need elaboration. They are perhaps rather obvious, but one only need examine experimental literature to see that appreciation of the two difficulties is not as widespread as is desirable.

The first difficulty mentioned above can be expressed otherwise by saying that if we define the experimental unit in an investigation as that complex consisting possibly of material, space, and time to which a particular input is applied, then there are no two experimental units that are alike. It is common to think that if we match individuals so that they are very much alike with regard to age, background, I.Q., and so on, that we may then treat two such matched individuals as though they are identical. One can of course see immediately that two individuals may be very much alike in those characteristics mentioned but one may have blue eyes and the other brown or one may have a low basal metabolism rate and the other a high one. Clearly, it is impossible to match two people so that they are identical. The rather widespread use of identical twins is an attempt to go in this direction. On the basis of present knowledge, the members of an identical twin pair will have the same genetic structure and, if reared in the same home, will have been exposed to very similar environments.

But without doubt one member of the pair will be different from the other by reason of chance occurrences, such as birth order, accidents of life, and a vast number of happenings, most of which may be of negligible importance. A partial answer to this problem, that no two experimental units are alike, is given by Fisher's principle of randomization. This very simple principle states that one should equalize experimental units as much as is feasible under the circumstances, and then randomize over differences which one cannot equalize over. I shall review briefly at a later point just what in my opinion such randomization accomplishes and what ambiguities remain after randomization.

The second fundamental difficulty may be expressed, using phraseology due, I believe, to Tukey, as the difficulty of inferring about the population of real interest—the *target* population. We may, for example, have done a comparative experiment on the freshman enrolled in a mathematics class at the University of Minnesota in 1959. But our interest in what happened to that particular group of people in that particular year is very slight, the good or damage having been done for this group. Our interest is in what should be done with the freshman mathematics class of 1960, 1961, and so on not only at Minnesota but also at many other places.

We may also be interested in other sorts of classes in somewhat different situations. Strictly speaking, we are never able to sample our target population. Even if we could draw a random sample of the target population as it is at the present moment, perform an experiment and analyze the results within five minutes, the target population is not that which we sampled. Just how different it will be is a matter of inference about the processes which lead to the target population. Such an inference is in my opinion impossible to validate in any strict sense. Two individuals attempting to infer the process, even if given the same data, will have different backgrounds and different views about what should be considered as relevant. They will in general formulate different models and will therefore obtain different predictions of the status of a particular future target population.

The logical difficulties inherent in this situation would cause an individual with no experience and no optimism to throw up his hands in defeat, and perhaps it is the existence of difficulties of this sort which delayed for so many centuries the real application of the experimental method to the problems of humanity. It is worth noting in passing that the logical difficulties I refer to are inherent also in the use of random sampling in sample surveys and the use of randomization in comparative experiments. In either case we utilize numbers produced by a device which has in the past given numbers in which we can find no system, *i.e.*, they satisfr as far as we can determine the Von Mises postulate of the impossibility of a winning gambling system. Also, in addition to our assuming that the random device will behave in the future as it has in the past, there is the difficulty of determining whether a sequence of numbers given by the device are random.

Any finite set of numbers will with sufficient examination be shown to exhibit features of regularity. The only relief for the statisician is to push the onus of the logical difficulty to as primitive a level as possible. A device which should be symmetrical with regard to physical characteristics is produced with as fine workmanship as possible, and the numbers it produces are examined by tests as good as we can invent. If these numbers pass our tests, we then proceed by assuming that the numbers it produces in the future will be random, though we may check our assumption at intervals both by examining the device for physical wear and by statistical tests. Essentially, these are only safeguards to buttress our act of faith that the numbers produced are random. Ultimately, the only justification for the whole procedure is that it has been shown to work, so we presume it will work in new situations.

It seems essential for clarification of the situation to distinguish two populations. One is the *target* population of Tukey, the population that we wish to "understand" and frequently to which we wish to apply our conclusions ; that is, to impose the inputs which our experiments have shown to be better. The other is the *experimentally accessible* population ; that is, the population which is available to the experimenter. In the case of agronomic experiments performed by an agricultural experiment station, the experimentally accessible population consists of certain areas, both on its own farms and on farms owned by cooperative individuals in the time period designated for the experiment. The target population may be all farms in a particular region which grow corn for the next few years. In a study on the effects of teaching freshman mathematics at Iowa State University by closed circuit television, by large classes and by small classes, the experimentally accessible population consists of the students taking freshman mathematics at Iowa State University in 1959, combined with the instructors, books, and so on available, combined also with the whole world complex in that interval. The target population consists of the students, the stndents' circumstances, and the world complex in 1960 and succeeding years. We can split the total inference into two parts :

(i) from the material used in the experiment to the experimentally accessible population at the time of experimentation and

(ii) from the experimentally accessible population to the real target population of interest.

In this paper I shall be concerned only with part (i) of the total inference, but before going into this it seems appropriate to say something about part (ii). We may on the basis of general knowledge say that the step from experimentally accessible population to the target population involves no difficulty. As a fairly clear case of this, suppose we are concerned with how to treat rocks of a particular geographical stratum in a defined area to get out the maximum amount of uranium We draw a sample from the population and try various methods. We then conclude that during the interval of experimentation the rock which we did not use has not changed, and that our methods of treatment are reproducible in the future whenever we wish. All of us would, I imagine, buy this inference; but I do not see how it can be given any tight logical basis. As a less transparent example in the field of education, our experimentally accessible population may be the population of freshman at Minnesota in the fall of 1960, say. Our target population consists of toe future populations of freshmen. We may have real difficulties in making the inference from our fall population in 1960 to other fall populations. I believe that in the last resort our only basis for making such an inference is our knowledge of characteristics of the respective populations or our knowledge that the changes in the past years have been inappreciable.

The difference between the experimentally accessible population and the target population may be of little concern in some purely physical situations, but as soon as one considers biological populations (and these include all population in any social science) the problem of spanning this difference is of major difficulty. In any experimentation there are real difficulties in defining the experimentally accessible population that one will use.

One can attempt to make the experimentally accessible population close, in some intuitive sense, to the target population and then encounter lack of precision. Or one can define the experimentally accessible population rather carefully so that much reduced variability is encountered. One will then have, hopefully, rather precise inferences to this population ; but one will have a large gap from it to the target population. There is no clear-cut answer on how one should define the experimental population. Narrowly defined populations tend to dismay the scientific man-in the-street and the statistical novice.

There is the almost irresistible desire to have conclusions of wide generality, but in many cases a broad definition of experimental population will lead to average conclusions which are not only very imprecise but also essentially meaningless because of interactions. Scientific life is no different from life in general in requiring compromises which turn out to be good.

Finally, it is important to note that in many uses of input-output relationships there are two distinct issues. We may be concerned with the effects on a population, which will of course be somewhat heterogeneous, of a particular input or stimulus applied to the whole population, as for example rigidly enforced state-wide standards for admissions to college.

Or we may be concerned about the effect of a particular stimulus on a particular individual. The bite of this situation arises when the particular individual is oneself or a close relative. We may well be satisfied on the best thing to do for the population and be completely unsatisfied on the best thing to do for the individual. This difficulty permeates such areas as medical treatment. One can envisage the occurrence of a situation in which an antibiotic or vaccine in prescribed for a whole group of individuals but which causes the death of a few of the individuals. The approach to the problem of best treatment for an individual is, I believe, essentially, but not entirely, a non-statistical matter and one to which objective validity of the sort that occurs in random sampling of finite populations cannot be claimed.

The basis for making such an inference is the placing of the individual in a reference set within which experimental data have been obtained and there is no evidence for nonadditivity of treatment effects. In considering whether an individual who asks for advice should take a remedial course in English, we have to use ideas of the following sort :

(1) Experiments have shown that such a remedial course is effective for a set of individuals,

(2) The individual we are now counseling does not differ from the set experimented with, as far as we can determine, in any attribute which could possibly have any effect on the issue.

The individual will of course differ from the experimental set ; he may for instance have been born in Cherokee, Iowa, with parents one of whom was of English origin and one of German origin, have been brought up in the Lutheran Church, have one brother ten years older than he is and one sister five years younger, have blue eyes, be six feet tall, and so on. Obviously, no individual with all these and other possible attributes was represented in the set of individuals experimented with, so we have *no* information on individuals like the one we are counseling, except insofar as we have experimental information that the effects of treatments are not related to differences in attributes of individuals.

The shorthand statement of how we reason for this case is that we rely on a demonstrated additivity of treatment and individual within a class of individuals. The placing of an individual in an appropriate reference set is very difficult and proceeds by trial and error, the most primitive form of an analytical survey. In a clinical problem, for instance, available measurements and information suggest that particular treatment is appropriate. The individual does not improve, and one then looks for attributes that my explain the absence of effect, as for instance that the individual has very high blood pressure. This whole problem is closely related to the question of standards.

The whole of the previous discussion has been on general difficulties of experimental inference. I shall now consider the drawing of experimental inferences about the experimentally accessible chosen by the population experimenter.

The Planning of Experiments

There are several texts on this general problem : Fisher (1935), Kempthorne (1952), Federer (1955), Cox (1958), Davis (1954), Villars (1951). There are also texts directed to educational research : Johnson (1949), Lindquist (1953), Edwards (1950). Each does a fairly good job of particular aspects of the general problem but none treats the whole problem with sufficient generality to be really effective, in my opinion. Perhaps the fact that I include my own book in the list and consider it to have considerable defects will palliate my criticism of all books.

What are the ingredients of the planning of an experiment ? In my view they are the following :

1. The strict definition of the accessible population.
2. The specification of treatments.
3. The specification of the process by which treatments are imposed on members of the population.
4. The specification of measurement procedures.
5. The specification of the inferential process,

The requirement that the experimentally accessible population be defined strictly is precisely of the same nature as the requirement that the population being examined by a sample survey be exactly specified. The latter is now entirely accepted. The need for this is apparent because our conclusions about the experimentally accessible population have a different status from our conclusions about other populations to which we may wish to apply the conclusions. One may, for instance, perform an experiment on children of faculty membees in a university town, and even though we may try to characterize the peculiarities of such a group by means of I.Q. tests, achievement scores, and so on we can be quite sure that this particular population has particular peculiarities which make extension of results to other populations more or less hazardous. The experiment may require a cooperative attitude on the part of school administration, teachers, and parents ; and the fact that these individuals are prepared to tolerate the experiment may well be a concomitant of particular attributes of the experimental group.

A regards specification of treatments, it is clear that treatment in the present discussion is a set of operations, inputs, or stimuli applied to a subset of the accessible population of individuals. An individual in this context does not necessarily mean a student or a class. It may mean the fifth grade of school X in the period October 1 to October 15, 1960. It is obvious, but still seems to me to need saying, that the set of operations must in some degree be repeatable not only with regard to the performance results of the experiment but also with regard to any use of the experimental conclusions. The degree of repeatability of the set of operations with regard to the outputs of interest must be susceptible to determination from the experimental data or from prior data.

One may, for instance, have a study of the effectiveness of group discussion in acquiring a particular piece of knowledge. It is obvious that a "treatment" of this nature is not well defined and not particularly reproducible, in contrast to a physical treatment such as "raise to a temperature of 80°C in two minutes and then maintain at that temperature for thirty minutes."

I wonder how often it has been said in the literature of educational research that treatment A was found to be better than treatment B, but where treatments A and B are so loosely described as to be poorly repeatable, and where the study does not contain any means of estimating degree of repeatability of treatments, or of estimating what may more generally be thought of as treatment error.

With regard to the process by which treatments are assigned to members of the experimental population there are two possibilities :

1. If the experimental population can be arranged in blocks such that there are no differences among members in the block, there is no point in doing anything but assigning the treatments haphazardly at one's will. However, there may be a case for randomizing over time in the application of treatments and the taking of measurements.

2. In general, since, we can never obtain memebers of the population who are identical, we may try to assign treatments systematically so that the different treatment groups are on the average, in some sense, alike, or we may randomize the assignment of treatments to members in some fashion.

The use of some sort of balancing in the application of treatments has the consequence that analysis is not at all unambiguous. The discussion by Fisher (1935) on systematic Latin squares relates to this point and should be studied. The difficulties Fisher discusses have led to the use of some sort of randomization.

The textbooks on design of experiments contain a whole battery of plans for the random assignment of treatments to "pieces" of experimental material, the completely randomized design, the block (complete or incomplete) design, the Latin Square design, split-plot designs of various sorts, and so on.

With regard to measurement procedures, the difficulties are common knowledge. The only statistical requirements are that the measurement procedures be reproducible to a measured extent and that they give independent results, no collusion between different measurements, and so on. The statistical viewpoint has essentially no contribution to the scientific question of whether the measurements are appropriate.

Choice of Frame of Reference for Inference

In all discussion modern statistical procedures, precision of estimates, distribution of sample statistics, tests of significance, tests of hypotheses, and construction of intervals which are to express our state of knowledge or basis for action, we have to consider 'with what population of repetitions are we concerned,' or, more concisely, what is the frame of reference or reference set ? Some on this quest in relation to what is a mathematically defined infinite population have been developed by one of my colleagues (Buehler, 1959). The problem is independent of, but closely related to, the problem of spanning the gap from the experimentally accessible population to the target population.

Suppose I experiment on the freshman mathematics class of the University of Minnesota in 1960, but I wish to regard the available individual-space-time combinations available to me as a sample from the totality of possible individual-space-time combinations, about which I wish to infer. It seems highly relevant to ask whether this accessible population can be regarded as a 'random' sample of whatever population you, the educational research worker, define. The experimental group has many possible antecedents in common and cannot in my opinion, be regarded as a random sample of any population you may wish to consider.

There are two ways out of this impasse. One is to think of the nature of the experimental group as a sample of a population with an assumed correlational structure, to imbed the sample procedure and results in the population structure, and then to apply some of the battery of statistical procedures, such as the method of maximum likelihood estimation.

The other way is to choose the smallest reference set which allows the drawing of conclusions. The conclusions are then well established for this restricted reference set, but the extension of these to an enlarged set is much more subjective and arbitrary. The general idea is that as a general basis fcr action it is better to have reliable knowledge about restricted sets of circumstances, and to have the uncertainty of extending this knowledge in the open, rather than to mix up inextricably the uncertainties of extending from the data to the accessible population and from the accessible to a larger population.

There is not in the present state of knowledge and art of statistics any way of deciding between the two approaches ; the choice seems to be a matter of personal taste. My own feeling is that it is better to infer about the experimental units actually used or randomly sampled, that is, to rely on derived models as illustrated below. It seems to me that the span from this population to any larger population is, in general, one on which statisticians, qua statisticians, are in no position to form reliable views, one in which a considerable substantive knowledge is required, and also one in which the total information available to the scientist cannot be expressed with reasonable reliability in termes of simple mathematical relations. Also, one cannot expect two scientists to possess the same knowledge and hence arrive at the same conclusions. Providing one is attempting only to infer about the accessible population, there is considerably greater possibility of all individuals agreeing, because this inference, like the inference in a probability sample survey of a population, can be made to depend largely on how the data were obtained.

The whole basis for the use of randomization is that it results in a conceptual reference set about which there can be no argument. The resulting inference is a restricted one but it is unassailable, at least in simple situations. Also, there is the point that much of the information one possesses before the experiment can be used to choose some restricted randomization. It seems to me essentially impossible to obtain an unassailable inferenee in any other way. Without the randomization reference set based on the randomization that has been used, every individual can reach a different answer, and it then seems impossible to me for statisticians to claim any special attributes for their conclusions. Also if one inspects the data to decide what model one will use in assessing the data, no objectivity can be claimed for significance levels, rejection of hypothesis ru les, confidence intervals and so on. I do not wish to say that one should not inspect the data, but I do think one should realize that there ls a gradation from the exploratory to the confirmatory type of experiment. I am concerned here primarily with the latter.

I have mentioned the choice of reference set as a problem, not because I feel that it present a problem to me, but because it clearly presents a problem in general as evidence by the existence of different models for ex' erimental data obtained in a particular way. It is also relevant to note that the use of the randomization reference set requires definition of experimental units before the experiment. The description of any randomized experiment should contain this definition.

The Randomization Reference Set

Let us consider the question of whether book A or book B is better in getting across to students in education the basic idea of a simple concept such as the variance of the mean of a finite sample. A situation and procedure could be the following. Suppose I have a class of N students, and that I present all the background material that I think is necessary in previous lecture periods. I then go into the class one morning, tell the students that I am going to give some of them a copy of the material in book A and others a copy of the material in book B. After they have studied the material for half an hour, I shall pass out a set of twenty yes-no questions for each student to answer in the remaining time.

The way in which I choose which students are to receive A and which are to receive B is to use a part of a table of random numbers in which I have general confidence. I can then adopt a very limited but unambiguous point of view that if individual i had been given A he would have yielded a score y_{1i} and that if he had been given B he would have yielded a score y_{2i}. So I have a conceptual population of possible responses :

		Individual		
Book	1	2	3	...N
A	y_{11}	y_{12}	y_{13}	$\ldots y_{1N}$
B	y_{21}	y_{22}	y_{23}	$\ldots y_{2N}$

This population is conceptual because if individual i gets A, he will give me the score y_{1i}, and I can never get score y_{2i} from him and vice versa. By assigning individuals at random to book A or book B, I have drawn a random sample of the numbers y_{1i} and a random sample of the numbers y_{2i}. Clearly, the average of individuals receiving A versus the average of individuals receiving B is an indication of the relative merits of A and B for this group. It is a simple exercise to evaluate the mean value and variance of the number we get. I shall give the manipulations in a form which is indicative of what can be done more complex situations.

Let

$$\delta^1{}_1=\begin{cases}1 \text{ if A is assigned to individual i}\\0 \text{ if A is not assigned to individual i}\end{cases}$$

$$\delta^2{}_1=\begin{cases}1 \text{ if B is assigned to individual i}\\0 \text{ if B is not assigned to individual i}\end{cases}$$

Then

$$\delta^1{}_1+\delta^2{}_1=1$$

because every individual gets A or B. By our procedures $\delta^1{}_1$, $\delta^2{}_1$ are random varibles with the following properties :

$$P(\delta^1{}_1=1)=P(\delta^1{}_1=0)=1/2$$

so that

$$E(\delta^1_1)={}^1/_2 \text{ and similarly } E(\delta^2_1)={}^1/_2.$$

If we let N=2r ta simiplify presentation

$$P(\delta^1_1=1 \mid \delta^1_{1'}=1) = \frac{r-1}{2r-1}, \; i \neq i$$

by which we mean that the probability that the i-th individual receive A, given that the i-th individual received A is (r—1)/(2r 1). This formula is true because when the i-th individual receives A, there are (r—1) individuals out of the remaining (2r– 1) who are to receive A, and the probability is equal for the (2r—1) individuals. Hence

$$P(\delta^1_1=1, \delta^1_{1'}=1) = \frac{r}{2r} \cdot \frac{(r-1)}{(2r-1)}$$

and also $\delta^1_1\delta^1_{1'}$ is zero unless both δ^1_1 and $\delta^1_{1'}$ are unity so

$$E(\delta^1_1\delta^1_{1'})= \frac{r(r-1)}{2r(2r-1)},$$

Also

$$\delta^1_1\delta^2_1=0 \text{ identically}$$

$$P(\delta^2_{1'}=1 \mid \delta^1_1=1)= \frac{1}{2r-1}, \; i \neq i'.$$

so

$$P(\delta^2_{1'}=1, \delta^1_1=1)= \frac{r^2}{2r(r-1)} =E(\delta^2_{1'}\delta^1_1), \; i \neq i'.$$

Then the obsrerved means for A and B are

$$\bar{A}= \frac{1}{r} \sum_i \delta^1_1 y_{1i}$$

$$\bar{B}= \frac{1}{r} \sum_i \delta^2_1 y_{2i}$$

$$E(\bar{A})= \frac{1}{r} \sum_i E(\delta^2_1) y_{1i}$$

$$=\frac{1}{2r}\sum_{i} y_{1i}$$

= the population mean under A

$=\mu_A$, say and similarly for B.

We can in principle determine any property of the means $\bar{A}$ and $\bar{B}$, because each is a linear function of random variables δ^k_i. The only difficulty is that the coefficients in these linear functions are *unknown* constants. If they were known we would have no problem and no experiment. The job is to infer something about $\bar{A}$ and $\bar{B}$ with knowing the y^k_i's. The variance of $\bar{A}$ is obtained as follws :

$$V(\bar{A})=E(\bar{A}^2)\left\{E(\bar{A})\right\}^2$$

Now

$$E(A^2)=E\left\{\frac{1}{r^2}(\sum_i \delta^1_i y_{1i})^2\right\}$$

$$=\frac{1}{r^2}E\left\{\sum_i(\delta^1_i)^2 y^2_{1i}+\sum_i\sum_{i'\neq i}\delta^1_{i'}\, y_{1i'}\right\}$$

so

$$=\frac{1}{r^2}\left\{\sum_i\frac{1}{2}y^2_{ii}+\sum_i\sum_{i'\neq i}\frac{1(r-1)}{2(2r-1)}y_{1i}\,y_{1i'}\right\}$$

$$=\frac{1}{2r}\left\{\sum_i y^2_{1i}+\frac{(r-1)}{(2r-1)}\left[(\sum_i y_{1i})^2-\sum_i y^2_{1i}\right]\right\}$$

$$=\frac{1}{2r_2}\left\{\sum_i y^2_{1i}\frac{r}{(2r-1)}+\frac{4r^2(r-1)}{(2r-1)}\mu^2_A\right\}$$

and

$$V(\bar{A})=\frac{1}{2r(2r-1)}\sum y^2_{1i}+\left(\frac{2(r-1)}{2r-1}-1\right)\mu^2_A$$

$$=\frac{1}{2r(2r-1)}\left\{\sum_i y^2_{1i}-2r\mu^2_A\right\}$$

$$=\frac{1}{2r}\sigma^2_A.$$

Where σ^2_A is the population mean square of the yield under A. This is of course equal to

$$\frac{1}{r}\left\{1-\frac{r}{2r}\right\}\sigma^2_A$$

in which the factor $\left(1-\frac{r}{2r}\right)$ is the finite population correction factor. Similarly

$$V(\bar{B})=\frac{1}{2r}\sigma^2_B.$$

Also the variance of $\bar{A}-\bar{B}$ is equal to the variance of

$$\frac{1}{r}\left(\sum_i \delta^1_i y_{1i}-\sum_i \delta^2_i y_{2i}\right)$$

$$=\frac{1}{r}\sum_i\left\{\delta^1_i y_{1i}-(1-\delta^1_i)y_{2i}\right\}$$

$$=\frac{1}{r}\sum\delta^1_i(y_{1i}+y_{2i})-\frac{1}{r}\sum_i y_{2i}$$

which is the variance of

$$\frac{1}{r}\sum_i\delta^1_i(y_{1i}+y_{2i})$$

which is equal to

$$\frac{1}{2r(2r-1)}\left\{\sum_i(y_{1i}+y_{2i})^2-2r(\mu_A+\mu_B)^2\right\}$$

$$=\frac{1}{2r}[\sigma^2_A+\sigma^2_B+2\sigma_{AB}]$$

where $\sigma_{AB}=\sum_i (y_{1i}-\mu_A)(y_{2i}-\mu_B)/(2r-1)$.

Now let us consider the estimation of variance. The observed mean square within A is to be found to have expectation σ^2_A and within B expectation σ^2_B. Hence as far asconsidering A or B alone we have, as is obvious, the usual finite sampling situation.

As regards the comparison of $\bar{A}$ and $\bar{B}$, the situation becomes reasonable if we can assume 'additivity' of treatment and individual so that

$$y_{1i}=x_i+t_1$$
$$y_{2i}=x_i+t_2, \text{ say,}$$

where x_i can be regarded in this instance as levels of ability. For we then have

$$\sigma^2_A=\frac{1}{(2r-1)}\sum_i (y_{1i}-\mu_A)^2$$

$$=\frac{1}{(2r-1)}\sum_i [x_1+t_1-(x.+t_1)]^2$$

$$=\frac{1}{(2r-1)}\sum_i(x_i-x)^2=\sigma^2, \text{ say,}$$

where $x.=\frac{1}{2r}\sum x_i$.

The variance σ^2_B then takes the same value, as also does

$$\sigma_{AB}=\frac{1}{(2r-1)}\sum_i (y_{1i}-\mu_A)(y_{2i}-\mu_B)$$

$$=\frac{1}{(2r-1)}\sum_i [x_i+t_1-(x.+t_1)][x_i+t_2-(x.+t_2)]$$

$$=\frac{1}{(2r-1)}\sum_i (x_i-x.)^2.$$

We would then have

$$V(\bar{A}-\bar{B})=\frac{1}{2r}(\sigma^2+\sigma^2+2\sigma^2) =\frac{2}{r}\sigma^2$$

and expectation of mean squares within treatments is σ^2. We therefore compare the squared difference of treatments means with $\frac{2}{r}$(mean square within treatments) or, if one wishes,

$$\frac{r}{2}\text{(squared difference of treatment means)}$$

$$=\frac{1}{2r}\text{ (squared difference of treatment totals)}$$

with the mean square within treatments. This is, of course, the usual analysis of variance.

	d.f.	S.S.
Between treatments	1	$\frac{1}{2r}$ (difference of treatment totals)^2
Within treatments	(2r − 1)	by difference
Total	(2r—1)	Total sum of squares of observations about overall mean

It is apparent from the above that since by Schwarz's inequality

$$\left\{\sum_i (y_{1i}-\mu_A)(y_{2i}-\mu_B\right\}^2 \leqslant \left\{\sum_i (y_{1i}-\mu_A)^2\right\}\left\{\sum_i (y_{2i}-\mu_B)^2\right\}$$

$$\sigma^2_{AB} \leqslant \sigma^2_A \sigma^2_B$$

the maximum value for the variance of $\bar{A}-\bar{B}$ is equal to

$$\frac{1}{2r}(\sigma^2_A+\sigma^2_B+2\sigma_A\ \sigma_B)$$

$$=\frac{1}{2r}(\sigma_A+\sigma_B)^2$$

which can certainly be estimated. Alternatively, the estimated variance that we use has an expectation larger than the variance because

$$\frac{2}{r}\left\{\frac{(\sigma^2_A+\sigma^2_B)}{2}\right\}-\frac{1}{2r}(\sigma^2_A+\sigma_B+2\sigma_{AB})$$
$$=\frac{1}{2r}(\sigma^2_A+\sigma^2_B-2\sigma_{AB})$$
$$=\frac{1}{2r(2r-1)}\sum_i[(y_{1i}-y_{2i})-(\mu_A-\mu_B)]^2$$

which is greater than zero.

This argument should, I believe, be very persuasive to all. There are of course many unresolved questions of tests of significance or hypotheses. This whole procedure does, however, provide within itself a test of significance of the null hypothesis that the numbers yielded by A and B for each individual are identical by the use of the permutation test. The basic idea is due to Fisher (1935), with some development by Pitman (1937) and Welch (1937). The idea behind the test is that there are (2r) ! / r! r! possible partitions of 2r entities into two sets of r entities each. If Fisher's null hypothesis stated above is true, then each partition leads to a value for any chosen criterion and there are (2r)! / r! r! equally probable values, all of which can be calculated. The number for the observed partition should not therefore be at all exceptional. If the possible deviations from the null hypothesis that we envisage would tend to make the criterion large, we can examine whether the value for the observed partition lies in the top 5 per cent of the distribution. If it does, we can consider the null hypothesis disproved at the 5 per cent level. Clearly the probability of the criterion lying in this part of the distribution. 'if the null hypothesis is true, is 5 per cent. So the test is said to be exact. We have ensured its exactness by the physical act of randomizing, provided only that our randomizing device gives random numbers. The scientist may wish for something more than this statement of degree of disbelief in the null hypothesis, but it seems entirely reasonable to some scientists and some statisticians to say : "Let is first examine whether there is any evidence aganinst the simplest hypothesis that whatever difference we observe is due to differences among the individuals over which we randomized. If this explanation is tenable, there is surely little point in pursuing the matter further, because anyone can with some justification accuse me of wasting my time. If this explanation is untenable my job is to characterize the situation in terms of some descriptive statistics with measures of reliablity." This I believe to be a paraphrase of Fisher's main theme for the past thirty or forty years, and in spite of some doubts which I shall express later, I still find the argument very appealing.

One can also examine, of course, the null hypothesis that A gives a score greater by five than B, or a score 50 per cent greater than B. The basis for this that a simple hypothesis of this type enables adjustment of data to a null hypothesis of no treatment difference, and if the adjustment is in conformity with the data one will then find little evidence after adjustment for significance of the difference of treatments. If it were supposed that treatment A is superior to B by a constant k, one could delimit the possible value of k which would result, after adjustment, in no evidence for a difference among the treatments. Or if it were supposed that A is superior to B in the ratio k to l, one could delimit possible values for k which would result after adjustment in no evidence for a difference of treatments.

Similarly, one develop tests for equality of variances within treatments and presumably, with a little thought, for other simple possible heppenings.

I shall only illustrate briefly the development of models for the more complex designs by the case of randomized blocks. The basis is as follows :

1. A pool of BP experimental units arranged in B blocks each of P unit
2. The selection of b out of B blocks at random
3. The selection of t out of T treatments at random
4. The selection of p = rt experimental units from each selected block at random
5. Random assignment of chosen treatments to chosen units within blocks

We can envisage a conceptual population of true yields Y_{ijk}, i = block, j = unit within block, k = treatment and observed yields

$$y_{ijk} = Y_{ijk} + \epsilon_{ijk}$$

where ϵ_{ikk} is an error of measurement and can then write as a population identity

$$y_{ijk} = Y_{...} + (Y_{i..} - Y_{...}) + (Y_{..k} - Y_{...}) + (Y_{i.k} - Y_{i..} - Y_{..k} + Y_{...}) + (Y_{ij.} - Y_{i..}) + (Y_{ijk} - Y_{ij.} - Y_{i.k} + Y_{i..}) + \epsilon_{ijk}$$

in which replacement of a subscript by a dot indicates averaging over the range of the replaced subscript. This equation can be written as

$y_{ijk} = \mu + b_i + t_k + (bt)_{ik} + e_{ij} + n_{ijk} + \epsilon_{ijk}$ in which terms are identified in order. The terms of this model have an explicit meaning, as, for instance, that $(Y_{..k} - Y_{...})$ is the difference one would observe if one could apply every treatment to every unit, and could take the average for treatment k minus the overall average. It is, then, the true effect of treatment k. The whole process of sampling from the conceptual population of possible yields can be represented by the model.

$$x_{i^*k^*f} = \mu + \sum_i a_i^* b_i + \sum_k \beta_k^* t_k + \sum_{ik} a_i^* \beta_k^* (bt)_{ik} + \sum_{ij} a_i^* \rho_{i^*k^*f}^{i*} e_{ij} + \sum_{ijk} a_i^* \beta_k^* \rho_{i^*k^*f}^{i*j} (n_{ijk} + \epsilon_{ijk})$$

where

a_i^* = 1 if the i*-th selected block is the i-th block in the population
= 0 therwise

β_k^* is defined similarly

$\rho_{i^*k^*f}^{i*j}$ = 1 if the f-th replicate of (i*k*) occurs on unit (i*j)
= 0 otherwise

Thus we have the observations as linear functions of random variables of known properties, and we can deduce properties of the observations and in particular of the analysis of variance of the observations.

This general topic has been explored extensively by myself and co-workers in the last eight years or so. (Kempthorne 1952, 1955; Wilk 1955a, 1955b; Wilk and Kempthorne, 1956a, 1956b; Zyskind, 1958; Zyskind and Kempthorne 1960.)

The Problem of Nonadditivity

The assumption of additivity mentioned above is that the observation on the combination of an experimental unit (defined to be the "piece" of material randomized over) with a particular treatment is equal to the sum of two contributions, one peculiar to the unit and the same for all treatments applied to that unit, and the second peculiar to the treatment and the same fo· all units to which that treatment is applied. In the case of comparing books A and B above with a group of students, it may happen that compared to book B book A is good for high-grade students and poor for low-grade students. Book would then interact with students. There would be nonadditivity of treatments (books) and units (students). This sort of thing can be expected, the less carefully the set of experimental units is chosen. One can, of course, take the point of view that unless the units are identical the responses, treatment A minus treatment B or $y_{1i}-y_{2i}$, will not be the same, but such a point cf view is sterile.

Examination of the completely randomized design with a treatment factor having t levels, each level applied to r units, leads to the following expectations of mean squares in analysis of variance :

Source	*d.f.*	*Expectation of mean square*
T	(t—1)	$\sigma^2+\sigma^2_u+(1-\frac{1}{T}-\frac{r}{P})\,\sigma^2T_u+r\sigma^2T$
Residual	t(r—1)	$\sigma^2+\sigma^2_u+(1-\frac{1}{T})\sigma^2T_u$

Here σ^2 is the variance of measurement error,

σ^2_u is the mean square among units averaged over all treatments,

σ^2_T is the mean square for treatments in the population of units,

σ^2_{Tu} is the mean square for interaction of treatments and units.

P is the number of units in the population (not necessarily all used).

If $\frac{r}{P}$ is small relative to $(1-\frac{1}{T})$, the expectation of mean squares for T and residual are practically the same and any increase of the former over the latter is an indication of treatment effects over the population of units used. But if $\frac{r}{P}$ is not small relative to $(1-\frac{1}{T})$ the mean square for T can be less than that for residual in the presence of positive σ^2_T. There would then be treatment effects and we would conclude there are none. The average variance of a difference of two treatment means is

$$\frac{1}{r}\left\{\sigma^2+\sigma^2_u+(1-\frac{1}{T}-\frac{r}{P})\right\}\sigma^2_{Tu}$$

which the residual mean square overestimates by

$$\frac{r}{P}\,\sigma^2_{Tu}$$

So we can see that there are circumstances under which treatment unit nonadditivity may affect us seriously. However, we have the general idea that interactions of units and treatments will be less important than differences among units themselves.

One can appeal to a Taylor expansion if the units and treatments can be represented by continuous variables. The requirement of additivity is then that some partial derivatives are constant, which is much less stringent than requiring that units be completely identical. The simples effect of nonadditivity is that the appparent error of treatment comparisons is overestimated, so there is a tendency for treatment differences to appear to be not large relative to error. I surmise that many experiments heve been discarded as inconclusive just on this account, when in fact the treatments produced different results.

Nonadditivities are a problem not only in the interpretation of an actual experiment but also in any nonstatistical extrapolation of the results to a target population, which is not, of course, experimented on. If one has experimented over a range of circumstances and finds essentially the same effects over this range, one may be confident, in a nonstatistical sense, about assuming that the obtained effects will hold under other circumstances. But if one finds interactions of treatments with groupings of experimental material, one can extrapolate only by discovering what we colloquially describe as an explanation and formulation of the nonadditivity.

One of the basic problems of interpretation of data is the removal of nonadditivities. There is a test for removable nonadditivity developed by Tukey. One can consider transformations of data, and at least in simple situations, the transformation which gives the highest F ratio for treatments compared to error more nearly achieves additivity. One can consider, after the fact of the experiment, the use of linear and nonlinear assumed models to determine if an explanation with less apparent inconsistency is achieved. Any such investigations would of course need to be substantiated in further experiments. Knowledge of the general problem and what can be done about it are still both rather naive, unfortunately.

The Reproducibility of Treatments

In the present context a treatment is an incompletely defined set of operations under the control of the experimenter. It is obvious that the description of the set of operations must be sufficient to permit another worker to reproduce the set of operations to a reasonable extent. Of course, no set of operations—for example, such as "teach Algebra 101 by means of closed circuit television"—is perfectly reproducible.

The scientist abstracts from the total set of operations he performs (which includes, of course, his whole life background) parts which he regards as relevant. The fact that the closed circuit television apparatus was manufactured by company Y or by company Z may not be at all relevant, though any such conclusion is an assumption which would itself require an experiment in order to be tested. I mention this because it is entirely possible that an experimenter comparing two sets of operations has a sub-operation peculiar to each which he does not even recall or think about which is the cause of the observed difference.

The experiment and statistics can lead to statements only about the total sets of operations. The abstraction from these of a particular part as being the scientifically relevant part is entirely a nonstatistical matter (cf. the use of placebos).

It is apparent, then, that even within a particular experiment the question of reproducibility of treatments—the sets of operations--must be considered. In physical and chemical laboratory experiments the problem may be a minor one, because one of the purposes of training in the area is the production of ability to perform reproducible operations.

In the area of educational research, however, the consideration of reproducibility of treatment operations with reference to results strikes me as being very important and essentially unconsidered. If one is concerned with the relative value of large classes and small classes, the operations "use a large class" and "use a small class" are very poorly defined and surely nothing like perfectly repeatable. One could define a large class as being one of 150 students, but one must have a lecturer, and one can be quite sure that different lecturers, or even the same lecturer on different occasions, will lead to results which are not identical. Any experiment on this topic must, in order to have bearing on the question of "large classes versus small classes," contain within it evidence on the repeatability of results over a class of repetitions of "large classes" and "small classes."

If all experimental units receiving each particular treatment receive it together, as for instance by all being taught in one way by one instructor, the only conclusion about any treatment difference observed is that it is attributable to the way of teaching or the instructor or partly due to each. One may well be satisfied that such a conclusion is the only possible one with the resources at one's disposal. It is, however, essential to realize that one is doing just this, and that the experimental conclusion is so delimited.

It may, however, happen that a treatment is only partly reproducible and that the differences among experimental units do not provide a fair basis to estimate the error of differences between treatments. This sort of thing can be illustrated very simply in the comparison of two means, say the mean of $x_1, x_2, \ldots, x_n$ under one treatment, and the mean of $y_1, y_2, \ldots, y_n$ under another treatment. Let us suppose that $x_1, x_2, \ldots, x_n$ have common variance σ^2, a constant correlation μ among pairs, and similarly for the y's. Then

$$V(x-y) = \frac{2}{n}[1+(n-1)\rho]\sigma^2$$

but the variance within either treatment is an estimate of $(1-\rho)\sigma^2$. It is apparent that the existence of such corrrelations can give an indication of the existence of real treatment differences when none exist. The F ratio, for instance, will be too large in the ratio $1+(n-1)\rho : 1-\rho$ which with positive ρ, due to common error of treatment applications, can be considerably greater than unity for particular combinations of n and ρ.

The basic problem in this, and indeed in all that I have discussed, is that a serious attempt must be made to ensure that the error variance by which we compare treatment means is fair, or, to use the technical phrase, unbiased.

Other Difficulties of Designed Experiments

I have already mentioned the problem of measurement error as one necessitating consideration at all times.

In educational research there is a problem of choice of method of analysis even at the most primitive level, which is indicated by the following case. Suppose we are interested in in the effectiveness of group discussion as a teaching device and that we have available a group of twenty students for the fall quarter of 1960. We will divide these students at random into two groups of ten. One of the groups is to experience organized group discussion and the other group is to have no group discussion. Whether such a vaguely defined "treatment" should even be exposed to experimental test is a question which I suppose which I suppose to be answered in the affirmative.

We might designate individuals by i (=1 to 60) and treatment by k (=1, 2) and envisage a population of passible scores at the end of the quarter of y_{ik}, and in line with the book example we could say that we have assigned students to treatments at random so the student is the experimental unit. It is, however, essential to realize that in this situation there are no numbers y_{ik}, but rather numbers y_{iks} where S designates the set of individuals who occur in a group with individual i.

It the group happens to contain a bright, stimulating individual, and if group discussion accomplishes anything, the values for other individuals in the group will be changed. Also, the value for that bright individual may be changed because the occurrence of other individuals may force him to think out problems to a more primitive level, and so on. These difficulties are such as to force us to consider the group as the unit of analysis even though the individual is the experimental unit.

Another rather generally occurring problem in educational research is the comparison of sequences of treatments. This problem also arises in long term nutritional experiments for land or animals, and in psychological experimentation. I shall content myself merely with expressing the view that there are in my opinion very few reasonably established ways of designing or analyzing experiments involving such considerations.

Concluding Remarks

I have attempted to describe what in my opinion is the present status and what are the more basic difficulties in experimental inference.

Looking back through what I have written, I have a feeling that the difficulties are so many and so intractable as to make experimental inference a very shaky process, and that a statistician cannot prescribe adequate recipes for even the simplest problems. On the whole, I think this is my position. Whatever contributions statistics can make to the whole problem lie not so much in the provision of cook-books by which problems are solved but in providing a framework and a way of thinking about problems. Good scientists know much of this way of thinking without even knowing the technical jargon of statistics. Perhaps statistics is taking over the role of philosophy for the working scientist. Perhaps, also, this is not entirely inappropriate, because the world is concerned to a large extent with experimental inference, and something must be done to clarify the process.

McHUGH : I would like to congratulate Professor Kempthorne on his most interesting paper. There are several issues it seems to me that invite comment. I shall focus on two.

First, the problem of nonadditivity; and then related to this, secondly, the matter of the "target population" vs. the "experimentally accessible population."

In view, on the one hand, of the clear-cut (in many cases one might say overwhelming) need for *randomized allocation* of units to treatment in order to avoid bias in the estimate of treatment effects, what, on the other hand, is to be done to obtain, for example, unbiased estimates of the error in the estimated treatment effects ?

Professor Kempthorne has demonstrated more fully elsewhere that rigorous statistical theory suggests just two solutions are possible in this problem of obtaining, for example, an unbiased estimate of error. In describing these I shall use two words from the title of his paper, viz., *design and analysis*. These two solutions are :

The Design Solution

Prior to the *randam allocation* of units to treatments,

perform *random selection*, that is, rigorous probability sampling in the sample survey design sense discussed here yesterday—from an existent finite population. In addition this population is to be sufficiently large in size so that it may be considered to be effectively infinite in the sense that the finite population correction is negligible. The first of these routes to an unbiased estimate of error I shall refer to as *the design solution*. Alternatively—

The Analysis Solution

Analyze the data on a scale such that there is *additivity* of units and treatments. I shall refer to this second solution as *analysis solution.*

The primary question that occurs to me at this point is: Although these two procedures are prescribable on the basis of theory, is either of them in fact *empirically* applicable.

Let us consider the design solution. This involves, you will recall, the actual sample survey probability selection of p out of P units.

Now, on occasion, a cooperative study of rare scope might bring this to pass. However, in my experience, the actual *random selection* of units from an existent, finite, but relatively large population *for the purpose of experimentation* is next to impossible, at least in biological research. Certainly in medical experiments "chunk samples" predominate, necessarily, I believe. It should be noticed, however, that although *random selection* may not be feasible, nevertheless *random allocation* ordinarily is applicable and is crucial for the internal validity of the experiment.

It would appear then that strictly speaking the design solution to the problem of obtaining an unbiased estimate of error is usually inoperative. However, before turning to the analysis solution, I would like to consider the design solution just discussed in the light of the issue: target population vs. experimentally accessible population.

I subscribe completely to the distinction Professor Kempthorne has drawn between the target population and the experimentally accessible population. However, perhaps a third population arises naturally, viz., that population of units which resembles the experimentally accessible population in all details *known* by the experimenter *to be relevant*. For brevity, I'll call this *Population Three*. Clearly Population Three is *not* —the *target* population. It is simply a sort of *inflated* experimentally accessible population, consisting, as I've said, of all units similar in every known relevant respect to the actual experimentally accessible population.

Let me illustrate. If a cancer biologist immunizes 40 mice of an inbred strain with tumor extract and finds that such a treatment (assuming his experiment possesses *internal validity*) results in a definite degree of resistence against challenge tumors, he is fully aware that his finding is *NOT* necessarily applicable, for example, to cross-bred strains of mice, nor to rats, cats, and so forth ; nor, in fact, to *humans* (his actual target population). In short, the *external validity* is, in this sense, quite limited. However, he does have in mind more than the population of 40 mice on hand, viz., a population which, in his judgment, is relevant to his experiment : for example, the totality of units that were in, are in, or will come into existence *which crucial resemble* the 40 units of his particular experiment, viz., *mice, inbred, female 30 days old*, etc,, etc. He may well insist upon making an induction, in some sense satistical, *to this population*, Population Three.

I would like to repeat that obviously this viewing of the units available as a sample from "Population Three" does not have *external* validity as a sort of sample survey procedure by fiat, so to speak, for probability inference to an extensive target population. However, as a matter of what is actually feasible in scientific experiments with respect to a *convergence* upon the target population in cumulative experiments, perhaps one may view the scientist's procedure - assuming may description to be correct-as a sort of stratified sampling approach, wherein, in a given area, the units used in *each of a series of cumulative experiments* correspond to a sampling from some stratum of a population which, by definition, is an approximation to the target population. Each new experiment attracks a new stratum, so to speak.

This viewpoint, which I think is held by many biological scientists, may permit of a solution to the problem originally posed, that of obtaining an unbiased estimate of error. In short, in all cases of scientific interest, perhaps one may realistically think of Population Three as large enough so that the finite population correction is negligible, for example, several thousand *mice*, which are *inbred, female*, etc.

Clearly, I'm viewing random selection and random allocation quite differently here. Actual random allocation is ordinarily possible, and crucial for the internal validity of the experiment. Actual random selection from an existent target population is ordinarily impossible for purposes of experimentation (though not for sample surveys per se, of course) but to view the sample of units on hand as representative in the probability sense of-*not* the target universe of units but rather-a conceptual universe identical to the sample in all "relevant" aspects seems to me not reprehensible.

Clearly, the foregoing is not the design solution originally mentioned. It is, in actuality, a device of analysis, not design, deriving its permissibility, if it possesses such, from the view the scientist necessarily takes of his units on hand.

Let us now turn to the formal analysis solution.

The analysis solution requires the determination of a scale on which there is unit-treatment additivity. Actually, convincing empiricial evidence that one has found such a scale in the analysis of data from any given experiment may well be extremely difficult to come by. The existence of information of this kind-viz., that on such-and-such a scale, unit-treatment additvity exists-may well be interpeted as the discovery of a *scintific law*, perhaps as hard to come by as, say an immunological law to the effect that "tumor extract generates cancer immunity."

To sum up : Perhaps the Population Three notion, viz., the utilization of the units on hand as having been drawn randomly from the scientist's *highly delimited* by conceptually effectively infinite universe is less of a statistical *tour de force* than the assumption that practicing statisticians are so frequently compelled to invoke of unit-treatment additivity.

Again, I would like to compliment Professor Kempthorne on an excellent paper.

LINDQUIST : I am sorry that I cannot invite any additional comments, as we have time only for the assigned discussants' reviews. Go ahead, Professor Gates.

GATES : The paper by Professer Kempthorne has been most stimulating.

As a minor moditification of the application of the randomization reference set to the one-way classification, assume that n_A ($n_A > 2$) and n_B ($n_B > 2$) predetermined individuals receive books A and B, respectively, such that $n_A + n_B = N$, as before. It can then be shown that.

$$V(\bar{A}-B) = \frac{1}{N}\left(\frac{n_B}{n_A}\sigma^2{}_A + \frac{n_A}{n_B}\sigma^2{}_B + 2\sigma_{AB} \right].$$

Under the assumption of additivity of treatment and individual this rcduces to.

$$V(\bar{A}-B) = \frac{N}{n_A\, n_A}\sigma^2.$$

Now the difference between the expectation of the variance that we use and the true variance now becomes.

$$\psi_A\, \sigma^2{}_A + \psi_B \sigma^2{}_B - \frac{2}{N}\sigma_{AB}$$

where $$\psi_A = \frac{1}{N}\left[\frac{N(n_A-1)}{n_B(N-2)} - \frac{n_B}{N} \right]$$

$$\psi_B = \frac{1}{n_B}\left[\frac{N(n_B-1)}{n_A(N-2)} - \frac{n_A}{N} \right].$$

The resultant equation is not as neat as Prof. Kempthrone's corresponding expression. It is interesting to note, however, that the expression remains positive even when n_A (or n_B) is at a minimum (2) and when σ^2_A and σ^2_B are greatly dissimilar.

While it is true that some treatments are currently defined so poorly as to admit nothing resembling repetition, even by the same person, I remain optimistic. Taking cognizance of the great complexity involved, it may be that gradually over a long period of time as knowledge of human interrelations accumulates, it will become possible to meaningfully and accurately characterize situations such as even the "group discussion" situation. Exactly what form these tools may ultimately take is not clear. My optimism undoubtedly takes sustenance from biological fields, where great strides have taken place in less than a century. Who would have imagined 100 years ago the detailed genetic predications now possible as the result of the cross of two mutant strains of *Neurospora*, such line clearly identified by genetic markers.

In contrast to group discussions, it is obvious there are some situations where even now it is possible to give almost identical treatments as, for example, a lecture illustrating one method of derivation of mean square expectations. By using various visual aids paraphernalia, as exemplified by closed circuit television, it would be possible to give the same lecture repeatedly under conditions as nearly identical as possible. Admittedly this does not resolve the problem of repeatibility of a given complex treatment by another individual.

KEMPTHORNE : I welcome Professor McHugh's comments. However, I do not consider that two solutions are presented to the problem of getting an unbiased estimate of error. There is one solution with two facets : design and analysis : Let us take the case of the cancer biologist with 40 mice from an inbred strain. The question I ask, as Fisher, I believe, asks in his *Design of Experiments*, is : On what basis can one get evidence for the effect of tumor extract with these 40 mice : The proposed answer is to use allocation of tumor extract to a random half of the mice and then to assess the results by some sort of analysis of variance or, in this case, a t-test. If there turns out to be strong evidence of an effect, the result is recorded in the literature with a specification, which the scientist and his intended audience consider adequate, of the origin of the mice and the experimental technique. Scientists will surmise that the results will be true for some larger set of mice, e.g. *mice, inbred, female, 30 days old,* etc., but the only basis on which they can do this is the possession of subject-knowledge, beyond the scope of any statistical formation.

Professor McHugh wants the result to be true for the totality of mice which ***crucially resemble*** the 40 units of his experiment. I imagine we would both subscribe to the existence of an unknown, completely deterministic picture of what is happening to the 40 units ; so I imagine we would agree that the results are true, within the limits of statistical error, for such a population. But what have we gained by making the statement that the results are true for a population crucially resembling the 40 units used ?

How do we establish that some other set of mice crucially resemble those we used ? Only, as far as I can see, by doing the same experiment with them and seeing if we get the same result. To do this we have to have an estimate of error in each case, so we seem to be back where we started, i.e., we need to have some basis for assessing the reliability of our conclusion about the 40 mice used or the population of Which the 40 used are a random sample.

There are various bases for attempting this, one of which I prefented in some detail. Another would be to assume that the 40 mice are a random sample from a larger population, but there are generally considerable difficulties in doing this : the 40 mice are certainly related environmentally and may be related genetically. Do we try to incorporate all such facets into our assumptions ? I believe that whatever knowledge we posses of this sort should be incorported in the design, for example by blocking ; but we should know the properties of inferential procedures for any such more complicated design before using it.

Professor McHugh agrees that there is a clear-cut (or even overwhelming) need to use random allocation of units to treatments to avoid bias. Bias is related to expectation over a population of repetitions, and I wonder what population of repetitions is relevant to determine if bias in estimation of treatment effects is absent. I believe that if a particular population of repetitions is appropriate for looking at one moment of a statistic, it is surely appropriate to look at other moments and other statistics. I wonder also what Professor McHugh means by "internal validity of the experiment," if not what I talked about. It seems to me that an experiment must have "internal validity," in some sense, before we can think about extrapolating its results to other situations, and this is What I was concerned with.

I was also interested in Professor Gate's comments. I, too, am optimistic about the achievement of better control of experimental operations, but I think experimenters in education have more difficulties to overcome than experimenters in biology, say. My remarks were based on reading several numbers of educational research journals, which led me to the view that quite insufficient concern is felt about this matter.

7

Educational Research in Universities

NICHOLAS A. FATTU
Institute of Educational Research
Indiana University

This survey is part of Phase I of a broader study of educational research in the United States.

I. THE NEED FOR EDUCATIONAL RESEARCH

American schools during the past century can claim a significant share in the development of the United States. They fused a variety of foreign nationalities, cultures, and creeds into a united nation, brought us to a position of world leadership, and gave us an unparalleled standard of living. Today's schools can claim credit for great improvement over those of even a generation ago. Reading, arithmetic, language arts, and other school subjects are taught far better. Students of comparable ability learn more and learn it faster.

Whenever data are available for comparisons, schools of today usually prove more effective. In these developments, educational research can claim a proud share. But measured against what our national responsibilities and resources call for, our schools are ineffective indeed. Until October 4, 1957, our position of technical leadership was rarely challenged directly, so far as the general public was concerned. Complacency was, and still is, reflected in grudging financial support of schools and certain anti-intellectual attitudes. The post-sputnik period was ushered in with a flood of criticisms of education by the press and certain other interests and groups. This scapegoat mechanism probably reflected the uneasiness associated with feelings of insecurity more than a basic distrust of public education. Science budgets were increased markedly, funds were made available for summer and other teacher's institutes in science and mathematics, and scientific societies for the first time began to exhibit a serious interest in the content and processes of public education. While these efforts are commendable, it is doubtful whether they will solve the underlying problem, since they are aimed at a few of the more prominent symptoms rather than at more fundamental causes.

In man's struggle to live happily in an increasingly complex world and to improve his lot, education has always been recognized as an important ally. In recent years the tremendous acceleration of scientific and technical development has left our public comprehension far behind. Unfortunately, it also left behind the comprehension of our leaders. The depletion of natural resources, particularly energy fuels, at the time of explosive population growth, coupled with the emergence of new social, political, and economic forces in Asia and Africa, has inevitably imposed a need for ever increasing complexity.

Education is needed in maintaining the supply of qualified and trained manpower not only in technology, but, more important, in those aspects of our world that make life worth living. Whether we like it or not, education will have to change markedly. Demands for ability, knowledge, and skill will have to be radically upgraded. This would be fine if all our pupils were geniuses, but when nature does not supply enough talented people education must make up the deficiency. Our national interest and well being demand increased efficiency of the schools. Development of more timely and accurate science and mathematics instructional materials, institutes for upgrading the knowledge of teachers, increased laboratory and library resources are certainly desirable but are "too little and too late." These stop-gaps take little cognizance of more basic problems of quality control in education.

Critics have suggested that the efforts of educators have not been such as to lend confidence in their leadership. Certain people, both outside and within education, have claimed that changes in education tend to come through accidental or incidental innovation rather than evolving in orderly fashion from a systematic body of organized knowledge. Educational problems are said to be solved by opinions, arguments, and debate rather than by facts and research. Frequently the very basis for research seems to be lacking.

It is the purpose of this paper to report some results of a pilot study of universities selected because they were outstanding in educational research. Even if these schools were taken as typical of all schools, it cannot be said that these criticisms are baseless.

II. PLAN OF THE STUDY

Information was collected and summarized around questions dealing with : kinds of studies and activities called educational research; the persons doing educational research—their background and preparation; the processes and procedures used; the incentives or climate provided by the institution to encourage research; the facilities and other support provided for educational research; the kinds of research that interviewees thought should be encouraged; the extent of cross-cultural or interdisciplinary exchange of promising ideas, tools, techniques, and data; the suggested means for improving current educational research; the goals and achievements of educational research; the feeling of educational researchers about the status of their work; suggestions for distinguishing what is good from what is shoddy in educational research; the organization of educational research within the institutions—kind, extent of formal structure, and services provided; recruitment, selection, and development of desirable graduate students; the extent of financial support of educational research. Of necessity, much of the information consists of opinions, impressions, and attitudes of the research workers interviewed.

The general plan was to do the pilot study by visits to the selected institutions. Data were collected by interviews; observation; and documentary analysis of college catalogs, available committee reports, etc. In the initial sample ten universities were selected on the basis of an index based on summed ranks of (a) judgments of three experts as to the amount and level of educational research done by the faculty, (b) number of research publications listed in the *Educational Index* during the period 1950-56, (c) graduate enrollment, (d) number of doctorates granted in education during the period 1950-58.

Interviews were begun with the dean and other responsible administrators. After responses to the dean's schedule had been obtained, he was asked to designate the members of his faculty who were doing, or had just completed within the last three months, research in education. Interviews were scheduled with these individuals and with those whom they designated. About one-fourth of the people interviewed were in divisions other than education.

Although responses were obtained in terms of a prepared interview schedule, these data are usually expressions of an impression, opinion, or the information that was on hand at the time of the interview. No reliability check was made. Over 200 people were interviewed. The summary below reflects the subjectivity of the data and the author's selection of materials. The discussion below does not cover all the questions included in the interviews.

III. SUMMARY OF DATA FROM DEANS

Dean's Questions

1. What is being done to provide a female research climate ?

What are the facilities; consulting, computing, and data

processing services ; clerical services for typing, scoring tests, collecting and summarizing routine information ?

Many things are done. These include :

(a) Providing facilities and conditions that encourage research by released time from teaching for research, adequate salary, promotions, research assistance, funds for research costs, consultative services, library and other necessary materials.

(b) Faculty committees that assist with mechanics of applying for grants, administering research budgets, and assisting specific research projects ; faculty interaction and communication that encourage rather than restrict identification and development of research upon significant problems.

(c) Administrative procedures that encourage the discussion of research problems and specific projects, the maintenance of channels of communication about research, the publication and critical review of research studies, the employment of a staff with research competence, and the provision of financial and social rewards for research of high quality.

(d) Employing and encouraging faculty members who strive for scholarship in their respective fields ; manifest genuine interest in and are productive in research; emphasize scholarship and research in their testing ; know actual problems or operations in education to which their research relates ; invest their primary research effort in studies of a basic nature; constantly stress the importance of their own, their students', and their institution's research ; continuously and realistically appraise their own efforts and competence as well as those of others ; do not undertake or direct research for which they are not competent ; continuously review and appraise the procedures used in training research workers and the climate of research present on the campus.

Comment

These are verbalized comments and are just what one would have predicted as responses to this sort of question. The fact that a dean may be fluent in giving many of these kinds of responses may not necessarily indicate that he vigorously supports such measures. The general impression was that the deans in all the institutions visited were sincerely convinced of the importanc of educational research and actively attempted to do something about it. In fact, because of the selection procedures used, any other pattern of response would have been most surprising.

However, the impression persists that even in these selected institutions there were wide individual variations in the extent and direction of administrative activity in support of educational research, but no attempt was made to quantity this impression. Some deans were content to pay verbal homage to the encouragement and support of research, and then get on either with their own research or with other tasks that are required of administrators.

The role of a dean actively promoting favourable public attitudes toward research was manifested by only one dean. This dean organized a Citizens' Conference in Educational Research where influential citizens and public officials participated—governor of the same, members of the legislature, the leaders of the various professional educational organizations. The need for financial support of educational research was vigorously promoted. This dean has also been a vigorous spokesman for educational research in his public appearances. His success in obtaining financial support for educational research should be of interest to those who complain about public apathy in the support of educational research.

So long as educational research is dependent upon the public for its support, it would be encouraging to see more effort directed toward informing that public as to the significanee and importance of educational research. Perhaps this may seem to be beneath the dignity of some administrators, but it is an essential function so long as we live in a republic.

Perhaps a digression into the support of educational research as compared to other research may be useful at this point. Business and industry, according to the vice president of Arthur D. Little, Inc., invests at least five per cent of its budget in research. Education spends less than five one-hundreths of one per cent for research.

Governmental expenditures for research are indicated, in millions of dollars, as follows :

	1950	*1955*	*1960 (estimated)*
Research and Development for National Security	871	1804	4572
Other	209	281	912

The Office of Education Cooperative Research Program budget for fiscal 1960 is about 3.2 million or about .03 per cent of the "other" research and development item. Budgets of state and city school systems for educational research are usually established at a much lower rate than this.

Discussions about educational research claim that potentially,

> It can test theory explicitly before costly expenditures are made for programs. It can take the practice out of trial and error. It can show how to produce a better product, more efficiently and with greater economy. Yes, educational research, like research in other fields, can save money ; it can increase the educational returns on our investments for schools. Sound educational research is desperately needed in these times to help produce better teachers, better schools, and better citizens. Investments in educational research undergird our national security and contribute to continued freedom of our people,

When one examines the budgets for educational research in relation to the needs for it, one is disappointed, to say the least.

2. How are the budget funds distributed among the functions of instruction, extension and public service, and research ?

Only five institutions gave usable data with reference to this question. These were distributed as follows :

	Institutions				
	A	*B*	*C*	*D*	*E*
Instruction	76.5	76.3	71.3	63.5	51.0
Extension and public service	2.6	3.2	3.2	7.6	16.4
Research	20.9	20.5	25.5	28.9	32.6

The reader is warned that comparisons between institutions are hazardous because the items included under each heading are not necessarily equivalent. The point that is clear, however, is that in the selected schools research receives a larger share of the budget than extension and public service. In schools not so well known for their research activity, this relationship is usually reversed.

3. How is faculty time assigned for research ?

It was thought that a better perspective might be obtained by obtaining time distribution data on all of the faculty.

Instrument A

	Time Assigned for Research						
	0%	*1-24%*	*25-49%*	*50-74%*	*75-99%*	*100%*	*Total*
Professors	21	7	7	3	5	2	45
Assoc, Prof.	10	4	5	1	2	1	23

Asst. Prof.	14	3	2	2	1	3	25
Instructors	7	7	0	0	0	0	7
Lecturers	1	0	0	3	1	0	5
Associates	2	0	1	0	2	3	8
Assistants	66	1	4	27	0	5	103
No Rank	2	0	1	0	0	0	3
	123	15	20	36	11	14	219

Institution B

Time Assigned for Research

	Under 25%	25-49%	50-74%	75-99%	100%	Total
Professors	27	5	1	0	2	35
Assoc. Prof.	21	0	0	0	0	21
Asst. Prof.	22	0	1	0	0	23
Instructors	53	0	0	0	0	53
Lecturers	3	0	0	0	0	3
Associates	1	1	1	0	3	6
Assistants	0	12	10	0	0	22
No Rank	0	0	1	0	0	1
	127	18	14	0	5	164

These data were collected under the assumption that schools which valued research most would make such provision in the allocation of faculty time for research. This may be a valid assumption in some schools, but it is unwarranted in other schools.

To make these data comparable one must make sure that the teaching load is essentially the same between institutions, i.e., a professor teaching seven hours would be listed in the zero column if the basic load was seven hours at his institution, and would be listed as having been assigned 50 per cent time off for research where the teaching load was fourteen hours. There are also such considerations as how demanding are the preparations for teaching and what are standards of classroom lecturing at the institution that must be taken into consideration. Among the universities visited, only the two distributions given above were regarded as sufficienctly comparable to warrant presentation of the data.

The data indicate that even in the institutions selected because of their research activities, most of the faculty members are officially assigned little or no time for research.

4. What is the research significance of faculty publications ?

Listings of faculty publications indicate that many of the publications are not research. They are usually editorials, book reviews, textbooks, or narrations about a point of view. The range of publications within an institution that might be called research runs between one-fifth and two-thirds, and this is irrespective of the level of the research published.

Comment on Dean's Questions

It was originally thought that the interview might be used as means of data collecting, and the interview schedule was designed to obtain data that were relevant to the importance that the institution attached to research as a faculty activity. Actual experience in doing the interviews suggests that this is essentially an exploratory activity that does not yield comparable data. However, it does provide suggestions as to the variations found among schools, and the need for reaching a common denominator before the data can be said to be reasonably comparable. In other words, these data reflect within-institutional characteristics ; it is hazardous to regard them as reflecting between-institutional practices except to a gross and unknown degree.

Summary of Data from Faculty

Individual faculty members were asked two sets of questions. The first set dealt with a case history of a current or a recently completed research project. This included :

(a) the background of the problem—what did it grow out of, its conceptual context or frame of reference ;

(b) specific questions currently being studied—deductions from the frame of reference, hypotheses being studied ;

(c) tools, techniques, devices, designs, tests, or methods used in collecting data, and nature of data collected ;

(d) analyses of data ;

(e) interpretation of findings in relation to frame of reference and their impact thereon—indication of revisions of frame of reference, new concepts, new hypotheses, questions, suggestions for new data, tools, techniques, instruments, devices, methods of procedure and analysis ;

(f) publications.

This block of questions was designed to identify the strategy and tactics used in educational research, and the likelihood that these would lead to cumulative development of systematic knowledge. A summary of this section is impossible within the time and space available. The impression of the author is that these case histories show a much more substantial basis for accumulation of knowledge than is usually evident in published research.

The second set of questions dealt with the faculty member's ideas on the question, what is educational research ? What criteria or standards does he use for distinguishing good from mediocre or poor educational research? What is adequate preparation of educational research workers—selection, course requirements, and research training experience? What aspects or developments in his field of interest appear to be most worthy for future development, or what trends seem to deserve support and emphasis in the future?

1. What is educational research?

"Educational research encompasses almost every sort of activity from the use of reference books by elementary school pupils to the most rigorous and systematic experimentation by research personnel."

"...Educational research is the activity that is directed toward the development of an organized body of knowledge about events with which educators are concerned. A scientific body of knowledge should enable the educator to determine just what teaching and other learning conditions to provide in order to produce desirable aspects of learned behavior among those who attend school. Learning conditions will have to be suited to the aptitudes and other characteristics of the learner."

"The kinds of problems dealt with by educational research include—development research, curriculum research, research related to sociological and economic conditions affecting education to [the individual's) teaching."

"Education research has ceased to exist. A large number of people are doing small studies, essentially amateur jobs that are not expected to influence anybody. Their value may lie in relation to [the individual's] teaching."

"The educational research spectrum includes:

"a. Fundamental research that could be equally well done in one of academic fields or behavioral science. The reward structure of universities is such that it gets you more than other types, and tends to crowd out applied research. Conclusions of this research should be relevant to educational method.

b. Work on educational principles, i.e., Brownell's work done in a classroom with classroom materials.

c. Development research designed to produce instructional materials in a form to be used in the classroom —the Illinois and Yale math projects and the MIT physics project.

d. Operational research or activity associated with the operation of an enterprise—selection test for candidates to veterinary college, surveys, etc., where no attempt is made to generalize."

"There is too little evidence-gathering on all sides."

"In education we need to look at the academic fields. The social wisdom of having all educational research done by educational researchers is questiona le. People who want to do theoretical or long continued research are better off in an academic field like psychology in terms of stimulation, where they can go as deeply as they want. . . . One must constantly balance a scholarly career against getting something done in education."

"What do we seek out of educational research ?. . .

"a. We seek to clarify as best we can the task that lies before us as educators. What are we trying to do ? This turns out to be an unusually stubborn and difficult question despite all the wrestling with it by educational policies commissions and others. Are we trying chiefly to sharpen the tools whereby our pupils can play their respective roles in life ? Or are we going beyond this to make them enlarge their vision as to what their roles might be ? How we answer these first questions determines how we answer the second group.

b. We try to discover how best we can achieve the ends we seek within the limitations imposed upon us by our communities, by the children who come to us, by those of us who teach. I wish to stress that because of these limitations education is an applied science and does not go on in a vacuum."

"We can do some kinds of research by *impoverishing* the situation. Thus we can study eye movements in reading by fitting the head into a frame and limiting the material which can be read. . . . so as to interfere as little as possible with photographing eye movements. Such experiments are good science, but my impression is that they have not served education very well because of their very impoverishment. They can tell us nothing about such important aspects of reading as how the child selects a book from the library . . . . The *literal* level of educational research is represented by rather plain and matter-of-fact studies of educational attainment, say the collection of norms on tests . . . . This' too, is useful but it has lacked something that we need.

"The enriched level of educational research requires that we study what is happening in school and community in some total fashion. Skill learning in the school may depend on the aspirations of different socio-economic classes, on the extent to which teachers understand these differences, as well as on teaching materials and methods."

"Educational research is conceived to include all forms of scholarly work aimed at discovering new knowledge at or making creative interpretations, organizations, or application of this knowledge. It may involve experiments in the laboratory, clinic, or classroom requiring considerable apparatus and equipment; it may be abstract and theoretical, demanding few facilities beyond paper and pencil."

Comment :

Educational research is different things to different people. The boundaries are those of the school or educational situation. Educational research appears to be willing to assume responsibility for all phases of scholarly activity associated with the educative process.

It thus includes :

(a) Carefully designed experimental studies that provide a critical test of current or proposed practices. Other types of studies, including surveys, may also contribute usefully when new approaches or techniques are used, but mass collections of data, not illumined by some guiding ideas, should be discouraged.

(b) Contributions of a theoretical, historical, philosophical, or integrative type as scholarly activities. Conceptualizations of areas of research to provide a general rationale or framework for studies that encourage a wise utilization of research effort.

(c) Critical reviews of research literature and summaries of issues and problems.

(d) Applied research, focused on local practices and policies, that is planned to stimulate interest in more fundamental studies, as well as to develop the school staff and illumine some immediate problem. This activity would be directed toward becoming operations or logistics research. The writing of textbooks, preparation of instructional materials, and administration of a school seem to be relevant activities when impelled by more basic considerations than those of the immediate situation.

Educational research seems to have rather fluid boundaries. One is forced to the banal, if not actually tautological, operational definition that educational research appears to be what educational researchers do.

The activities of researchers interviewed in the pilot study exhibit a different picture from that reported by Ryans as typical in the activities of research offices. It is activity of these rather than the typical researcher that the definition might stress.

2. *How does one distinguish between good and poor research ?*

Items listed below that are not in quotes have been edited

to reduce their length. An attempt has been made to preserve the intent of the interviewee.

This distinction usually emphasized an appraisal of the product or end result rather than the process by which it was rached. In research, however, one cannot necessarily predict that a given study will yield positive results, hence the level at which the researcher works also needs to be considered. Essential distinctions in the research process were made in terms of the level at which a professionally mature researcher could be expected to work. Sometimes the mature research worker himself did not function at his level, especially if he was on unfamiliar ground, in a hurry, or disturbed by the results.

A good study puts us ahead of where we are now, tackles problems not handled by peers, solves problems that others have failed to solve. A good study makes a difference in educational practice if the potential applications are taken seriously. A good study is imaginative, ingenious, and productive of new approaches, new ideas, and new data. A good study fits into a pattern of long range work. It has antecedents and consequents, and the total result is increased understanding of a field as a result of the accumulation of studies.

A good study is carefully designed and planned. It identifies a definite problem. All parts of the procedure are relevant to the question being studied – data collected, analysis of data. The interpretation of findings or meanings of results is directly related to the organization of the study and the procedures used. The results are also directly related to the conceptualization used, and may suggest new data and new concepts.

A good study is aimed at discovering truth, not at supporting, a current or proposed practice. It deals with more general and universal aspects of questions that concern education. The goal is not to find a quick solution but to develop tested principles. Results of a good study can be communicated to peers working in the same area.

A good study is appropriate to the level of development of its field and to the questions asked. Education is an enormous public enterprise engaged in a form of mass production. It is impossible to aperate on this scale without systematic quality control, for without quality control we don't know where we stand, and we cannot correct the weak spots. A program of quality control involves systematic and continuous collection of facts on pupils, including long term follow-up of graduates. Data would include tests but would also include data on motivation, socio-economic background, level of aspiration, emotionality, etc. Operations research tells the school about its raw material and about its output. Operations research and quality control methods could be applied to operational data.

Poor studies consider an unimportant problem, are improperly designed, are over-generalized, or improperly done. They include trivial studies or those that have been done so often that there is no use doing them again—correlations between ACE, high school ranks, etc., and college grades.

In educational research the objection to a study is not that the data are not as precise as laboratory experiments, because one recognizes that education data have a high variability built into them. The objection is that such studies are often *ex post facto*; i.e., "what happens to high ability youth ?"

A poor study doesn't account for enough of the variance, has an insufficient number of independent variables, or permits little identification of variations. Such studies are often repetitious and naive, often definitely clerical in level of manipulations.

Clear, precise studies of learning under various treatments appeal to natural scientists. But many studies lack a central problem, or have no theoretical formulation and no comprehension of why they may be important.

Many education studies are trivial or axiomatic. Investigators often just pick up variables that happen to be around, precise identification of dependent and independent variables is lacking, and they often miss variables entirely or fail to name them.

Poor studies are illustrated by some of those in the productivity of groups. One gets a correlation of .70; one can choose any variables and still get the same correlation. The basic failure is in not understanding what the relevant variables are.

Comment :

Distinguishing betwen good and poor research on an overall basis is difficult to accomplish and to communicate. Since the quality of studies differs in many characteristics rather than on an all-or-none basis, general distinctions properly lead to substantial difference of opinion. Within his own frame of reference, a researcher can readily make distinctions between good and poor studies. Difficulty arises when he attempts to communicate these distinctions to others. The case histories of research projects given by the intervewees appear to exhibit sufficient similarity in level of scholarship, persistence, conformity to criteria of intellectual integrity, knowledge of the field, command of research techniques, tools, and methodology, etc., to warrant an attempt at communication. To succeed would require that the distinctions be reduced to some definite bases. A set of evaluative criteria could be developed and each illustrated by specific examples. These materials could be submitted to a jury of peers for appraisal. Resulting data could determine feasibility of the attempt. If the data exhibited desirable characteristics, further study using a scaling technique miget be pursued. Such an effort would be useful during the training of research workers, or in conjunction with their training. Editors of journals and other professional publications and administrators of research grants might also find these criteria useful. However, competently trained researchers could probably spend their time to better advantage pursuing their own research rather than evaluating that of others.

3. ***What is adequate preparation for educational research (selection, courses, and research experiences)?***

Selection : Traditional criteria for selection such as high intelligence and a high undergaduate record alone do not provide a desirably accurate or comprehensive base. Other predictors that should be investigated include originality, creativity and imagination, curiosity and enjoyment of intellectual exploration, independence of investigation and thought, persistence in carrying on projects to completion. Motivation toward research is very important and should be considered.

Courses : Comments favored the following: The program of training research workers should take account of the students' abilities and interests, and the institution's faculty and other resources. There might be some combinations of the following components in course offerings : a set of service courses wherein the faculty discusses its conception of the theory and practice of education, the body of knowledge in education and from the behavioral sciences bearing on the areas of concentration, the research techniques and procedures used in this field; a series of seminars where professors describe their research projects and where participants actively appraise and criticize; a series of opportunities for students to formulate and test their own research approaches. The emphasis appears to be put not so much on courses as upon capability of the faculty, institutional climate, and resources for research.

Several interviewees doubted that the greater the student's mastery of statistical and other tools the more effective he would be in research, or that the greater his scholarly knowledge of the field the more likely he would be to contribute to that knowledge. They also doubted that the value of theory increased as it become more formalized and detailed. The importance of these elements was not belittled. "Statistical competence, scholarship, and theoretical sophistication are all important in research.

The point is that each of these should be means toward

the end of contribution to knowledge, not ends in themselves. The danger is that the individual will become so enamoured of statistical techniques that they largely determine his research decisions,...

The danger is also that so much time will be spent in mastery of these means that too little time will be left for other experience crucial to the development of a creative researcher.." "Competence in tool subjects or skills such as mathematics, foreign languages, electronics, physiology, etc., should be required of individuals where and as needed, but required in depth rather than as across the board hurdles that all must meet."

Others indicated that "education is not set up to train educational research workers. If one is training for research, he needs to have the student in a research atmosphere. Research people come in bunches like grapes. In schools of education, a research person is unhappy—he needs facilities, library, assistants, equipment. The student is put into a curriculum and experiences isolated from research contact, loaded up with course work." Still others indicated that graduate training in education is directed toward a professional goal, usually teaching or administration. Research is often only a peripheral activity. There is no graduate school that specifically prepares professional educational research workers.

Another suggests that "successful educational research does not reflect any particular training. Select twenty-five people doing educational research, find their career route and you will note that background of training makes little difference. The problem is of recruitment and seduction of competent people, rather than of the training program. Study the jobs – what are the roles in which educational research has gotten performed— Cronbach, Tyler, Brownell, Neal Gross. The job role is more significant than training when you have oustanding people."

Research experience in training : No dissents were observed with respect to the importance of research experience during training. Most people assigned this phase primary importance,

Some cautioned that the significance of this experience depended on the nature of the faculty, their interests and productivity, upon student interest, and upon student-faculty compatibility.

"Education for research must do more than develop competence in desiging, executing, and interpreting studies. Developing such competence is important, but much more so is the development of the individual's creativeness – his ability to discover new relations, to reformulate or systematize known facts, to devise new techniques and new approaches to problems."

For the teacher or administrator "one can specify a range of problems with which he will have to deal and the substantive knowledge, methods, and techniques likely to be relevant. Standardization of preparation for such jobs has much to recommend it. In contrast, research is always concerned with search for new knowledge and there are no clear-cut rules for finding it...It is our belief that the education of the research student must be largely in terms of the interests and aptitudes of the individual."

"In training for research we should be interested in developing researchers who know how to do research and who continue to do so. One is most likely to sustain a productive research career if he has found research satisfying."

"The task of the researcher is not mainly that of designing a study, collecting data, analyzing results, or drawing conclusions...this is not what makes the difference between run-of-the-mill and significant work." Confirmatory activities constitute but a small part of the process of active research, and mostly in the terminal paase."

"Creative activities are often informal, sometimes illogical, and far from neat looking. They include a great deal of floundering, pilot studies, exploratory research. Numerous leads and ideas are developed. Most of these are rejected outright, some are followed up.... If an idea followed happens to be poor, a lot of time is wasted. If it happens to be good, the researcher may make a positive contribution. Between the idea and the contribution lie a lot originality, intuition, persistence, and hard work. It is this sort of activity that comes first in time, or there is little worth processing by the confirmatory activities. The job is rarely finished by doing an experiment and finding significant differences. Making a contribution is a process of continuous work during which ideas change and develop."

The following comment provides a summary to the matter of training for research :

"Central to education for research is a faculty which itself is actually doing research. With such a faculty formal course work can usefully supplement the development of researchers tnrough the internship. In the absence of such a faculty and thus the absence of meaningful internship, preoccupation with the improvement of courses offered or of various formal requirements can contribute little to what is crucial to research training."

CONCLUDING STATEMENT

Data reported here are inherently incomplete in terms of giving a picture of the current status of educational research. This was recognized in the original plan. Phase II of the project will attempt to get comparable data from all institutions that grant a doctorate in education. The pilot study was done to obtain an idea of points that might be significant within the domain of educational research, and to explore feasible means of obtaining comparable data.

Outstanding institutions were selected in order to observe the state of the practice at its best. The complacency observed was disturbing. To be sure, there were many examples of capable and dedicated workers. However, the nondiscriminating kinds of activities currently carried on under the name of educational research tend to bury these with the mediocre.

The physical, biological, medical, and agricultural sciences have reconized that their effectiveness is based on a constant harvest of new knowledge. Innovations are systematically developed from an ever increasing body of knowledge and rigorously tested for effectiveness. Contrast this with the usual practice in education. The plain fact is that the formula of innovation by accidental discovery or improvision is completely antiquated.

Historically, the older sciences began and were supported for centuries by the work of amateurs. Their significant period of growth, however, began only when the amateur ceased to play the major role. Adding to the basic fund of knowledge in education is rapidly approaching the stage where casual part-time effort is not enough. Education will begin to approach its proper level of efficiency only when we recognize that the problems of effectiveness are scientific and technical, not political. Only by inspired, sustained, and systematic research in education similar to that which has graced the older science can education become truly effective. In that research the membership of Phi Delta Kappa must be prepared to play a proud part.

8

Federal Government and Educational Research

HERBERT S. CONRAD
Office of Education
U.S. Department of Health, Education, and Welfare

Before embarking on my topic, it seems fitting to commend Phi Delta Kappa and the University of Virginia for their initiative and good judgment in sponsoring a symposium on educational research. Now, more than ever before, the significance of education as our basic national resource is receiving recognition. Now, more than ever before, the advancement of education *through educational research* becomes a paramount national goal.

I. CONTRIBUTIONS THROUGH NATIONAL SURVEYS

The Federal government (principally through the Office of Education and Bureau of the Census) conducts numerous surveys which are basic to certain types of systematic research. Some of these surveys provide an *inventory* of response units or basic sources of information. Thus, the Office of Education issues annually a directory (officially entitled *Education Directory, Part 3 : Higher Education*) which lists the institutions of higher education in the United States ; the Office also issues annually (as *Education Directory, Part 2*) a list of "superintendents of country, supervisory districts or union, city, town, and urbrn schools"; and it also issues (at intervals of about 5 or 6 years) a directory of secondary schools. The Bureau of the Census, in its Governments Division, periodically brings up to date a list of all the local school districts in the United States (currently about 50,000).

These various lists are an indispensable and invaluable reference source for studies based on scientific, sysmatic samples of collegs, schools, etc. They also are a means of obtaining samples of other important educational groups ; to cite only one example, the sample of teachers investigated in a nationwide survey of *The Beginning Teacher* (Office of Education Circular Oo. 510, 1958) was obtained from a sample of school districts drawn from the Census list.

The various lists or directories invite and facilitate national as (distinguished from sectional or local) studies, based on scientific sampling ; thus, the national survey of talent in grades 9-12, being conducted by the University of Pittsburgh with the aid of funds from the Cooperative Research Program of the Office of Education, is based on a sample drawn from the Office's directory of secondary schools. Of course, the national lists and directories may also be used for more restricted studies, covering only a particular region or State, or a restricted selection of units (such as small high schools rather than all high schools, junior colleges rather than all colleges, etc.).

Other national surveys by the Office of Education serve educational research by providing basic background data—such as information on enrollment, on teaching staffs, on expenditures per pupil, on financial aids (scholarships and loans) available to college students, on sources of income of schools and colleges, etc. These surveys frequently serve to identify, or give dimensions to, problems— which is the first step in any rational research methodology.

Thus, a national survey of financial aids for college students demonstrated the need for remedial action in this sector (Title II of the National Defence Education Act of 1958 is responsive to this need). Data from the Bureau of the Census and from other sources on the number of children in public and private schools point to a need for investigating closely the factors resposible for the study rise in the proportion of private school pupils. Illustrations could be further multiplied.

Most of the Federal surveys in education are conducted by means of questionnaries. The questionnaire has perhaps been abused as frequently by its critics as by its users. For certain types of study, the questionnaire is by far the most economical, and indeed the only feasible, instrument available. The Federal government has taken the lead in fulfilling the basic methodological requirements for the successful use of questionnaires for national surveys. Evidence of the Government's interest in this domain is the establishment, in the Executive Office of the President, of the Office of Satistical Standards, one of whose functions it is to pass on the soundness of all (or virtually all) questionnaires distributed by any agencyof the Federal government.

A good idea of proper questionnaire procedure may be gained from the steps in a variety of surveys conducted by the Office of Education (not each of these surveys incorporates, with equal strength, all of the steps indicated below). The outline given below does not pretend to constitute a model for all questionnaire surveys in education ; but some elements, at least, of the outline may be regarded as useful contributions to methodology in this field.

One of the first steps required in any questionnaire survey is that the investigator.

(a) define clearly the terms and concepts enterning into the questionnaire, and

(b) effectively communicate these definitions to the respondents.

Some elaborate steps have been taken been taken by the Office of Education to assure the achievement of these two ureqirements in the field of State and local school accounting. The general procedure included the following five steps :

(1) Definitions were drawn up by members of the staff of the Office of Education - with due reference of Federal, State, and local manuals, educational glossaries or dictionaries, and current educational usage (in various report forms, questionnaires, school system reports, etc.).

(2) National and regional conferences were held, in which the definitions prepared by the staff were discussed, modified, and refined. Participation in these conferences varied according to the particular area under consideration.

Thus, in developing the definitions for *The Common Core of State Educational Information*, the participants included, in addition to staff members from the Office of Educatior, representatives from all the State departments of education, from the National Education Associrtion, the American Association of School Administrators, the Association of School Business Officials, and the Council of Chief State School Officers—as well as officials from private associations representing nonpublic schools, such as the National Catholic Welfare Conference, the Headmistresses Association of the East, etc. Literally hundreds of interested, competent persons participated in the conferences-including persons who would themselves be responding in the future to questionnaires incorporating the definitions arrived at.

(3) The proposals and recommendations gleaned from the conferences were collected and edited by the Office of Education staff, then submitted to a final national conference, and then sent for review to the various educational associations particularly concerned.

(4) A final set of definitions was established, and published in the from of a "handbook." (These definitions are utilized by the Office in its surveys of State and local school systems.) To date, three handbooks. together with a supplement, have been issued.

(5) Copies of the handbooks have been widely distributed to appropriate persons, and the handbooks have been placed on sale, at low prices, at the U. S. Government Printing Office.

To be sure, it is not always possible or necessary to adopt a procedure as elaborate as the one outlined above. The spirit of the procedure, however, deserves widespread emulation. The spirit of the procedure not only helps insure the adequacy of the definition, *per se*, but also enhances the acceptability of the definitions after issuance, and makes an effort to disseminate the definitions widely.

Definitions are, of course, only one of the first steps in the methodology of a questionnaire survey. *Obtaining a response*—on all the items, from practically all the respondents—is another step, and it presents special difficulties when (as in the case of questionnaires from the Office of Education) those receiving the questionnaire are free to respond or not, as they see fit. Here enter such elements as the reputation and responsibility of the investigator, the significance of the data which are requested, the reasonableness of the burden imposed on the respondent, the timing of the survey, and, last but not least, the skill and pertinacity of the *follow-up efforts* by the investigator.

In general, it has proved feasible for the Office of Education to set very high standards for itself with regard to completeness of response. Ordinarily, more than 90 per cent of the questionnaire recipients—sometimes even a full 100 per cent—respond.

This very high response rate obviates the need for special studies to evaluate possible response bias among non-respondents. Follow-up procedures include not only routine form letters, but also special-appeal lettters to various subgroups of the total sample (a separate letter for each subgroup), and individual, personal letters when necessary. Use is also made of telegrams, telephone calls, and occasionally (though rather rarely) of field visits. (Lack of a regular field staff for statistical studies makes the use of field visits impractically expensive except in cases of unusual need.)

A special feature of methodogy in questionnaire surveys of the Office of Education is the care taken in the ***verification of responses***, when such verification is possible Sometimes the possibilities for verification are considerable.

Thus, in a biennial survey of faculty and other professional staff in institutions of higher education, at least five sources of information are ordinarily available for purposes of check or verification, and are used to the extent needed. The first of these sources is the report from the same institution in the previous survery (two years earlier); if any large, unexplained change is reported, further investigation is made.

Another source of information is the data in the questionnaire itself; this may be termed the check by "internal consistency," in which unusual combinations of data are found suspect. and are corrected or verified by reference to other sources. A third check is obtained by comparing the faculty data with data obtained in *other* questionnaires from the same institution.

Thus, we sometimes find that no faculty members are reported as giving instruction in extension; yet the registrar (in a report of the Office of Education on enrollment) has recorded the number of extension students, and the comptoller (also in a different questionnaire) has reported on expenditures for extension instruction. Obviously, here the failure to report on faculty members giving instruction in extension represents an error. A fourth resource for verification is the college catalog, and other printed materials (such as *American Colleges and Universities*, published by the American Council on Education). The final resource, of course, is the institution of higher education itself, which may be asked to correct or verify figures brought into question by one or another of the sources of information cited above.

As mentioned in connection with the definition of terms and concepts, it is not always possible or necessary to adopt as elaborate a procedure as the one indicated above. Nevertheless, *some* checking or verification of responses is always desirable. A planned procedure for verification is a regular part of a typical questionnaire survey by the Office of Education.

The type of verification described above goes considerably beyond so-called "machine checking" or "machine editing." i.e., the use of machines to verify additions, detect abnormal differences or ratios between figures, etc. Machine editing is generally limited, by its nature, solely to the information on the given questionnaire.

Hence, it can execute only the "internal consistency" check. The historical check by reference to responses of a previous year and the check by reference to other sources of information are generally not possible or feasible.

Further, machine editing suffers from the fact that, for practical reasons, the returns can be machine-processed only after a large "batch" has accumulated. Ideally, however, the check or verification of returns should proceed on a prompt, day-to-day basis, in order that letters of inquiry regarding dubious or unsatisfactory aspect of the returns may be addressed to the respondents at once. It requires mention, finally, that machine editing can, in any event, accomplish only half the job; for while it can *detect* certian kinds of errors, it does not *correct* them. Regardless of these limitations, machine editing does permit a quick, terminal check or re-check of certain aspects of the data: and is being used by the Office of Education for this purpose.

SUMMARY

The procedures discussed above appear to represent the main contributions of the Federal government to educational research methodology in the field of national surveys. By way of summary, these features include :

(1) the development of inventories of response units or basic sources of information, which invite and facilitate national studies based on scientific sampling;

(2) the providing of basic background data which are of service to many investigators, and which frequently serve to identify or indicate the magnitude of, various educational problems;

(3) the development of a procedure for the definition of basic terms and concepts which, first of all, capitalizes on the interest and knowledge of a large number of users and suppliers of daia, and second, helps to assure both the better understanding and the wider acceptance of the definitions finally arrived at;

(4) the obtaining of very high response rates by procedures which are persistent, adaptive, and not very expensive; and

(5) the careful and extensive verification of returns.

II. CONTRIBUTIONS THROUGH RESEARCH IN THE ARMED FORCES

During World War II, and unparalleled upsurge of research on personnel took place in the Armed Forces. Most noteworthy from the viewpoint of educational research methodology was the research on the success or failure of individuals selected for special training in service schools. For some time, it had been recognized that the lack of *adequate criteria of "success"* constituted a grave shartcoming of most studies of personnel selection and training.

One of the most significant methodological advances was achieved in this area. The criteria employed in the Armed Forces' research naturally included marks earned in the service schools; these were too convenient and useful to be ignored. But the criteria also frequently included—to an extent greater than customary in educational research—formal measurements on *speceific performance criteria,* such as the ability to disassemble and reassemble part of a complex mechanism, the ability to hit a target under specified favorable or adverse circumstances, etc. Moreover, the criteria extended *beyond the school experience into actual working or combat situation*—where the ability to *apply* what one has learned gains its proper importance.

Very few selection or training procedures in education today are subjected to such practical, realistic check. Perhaps the circumstances in the Armed Forces presented favorable features for the study of "practical" or "ultimate" criteria: large numbers of persons were available for studs; the variety of jobs was comparatively limited; and funds for research were sufficient.

The handicaps of civilian research, however, may be too readily exaggerated. In the writer's view, too little attention has been given to the implications of the Armed Forces' research, and to the possibilities of transfer from this research to peacetime studies. Apart from the impact of the Cooperative Research Program (discussed at a later point in this paper), the organization and financing of educational research do not appear to have changed significantly since World War II. Figuratively speaking, it seems that the rapid demobilization of the men of the Armed Forces carried with it the liquidation of the Armed Forces' methodological advance in educational research.

Two operating procedures employed by the Armed Forces are of interest for their applicability in the selection or identification of exceptional individuals for research studies. At the one extreme is the method of rapid screening by means of a very short, quickly scored questionnaire or test. Such screening, of course, is not as reliable or valid as selection based on longer or additional measurements; but it can reduce considerably the number of individuals to whom the more expensive procedures need be applied.

At the other extreme is the "pesonality assessment" procedure, by which a person is observed for several days in a variety of semi-controlled, yet more or less natural, situations (including a generous number of interpersonal contacts and relationship and some situations involving stress); various tests, both objective and projective, are also administered. Observation is by a team of practiced experimenters. Evaluation of behaviour is quantitative w here possible, qualitative where appropriate. So far as research is concerned, the "assessment procedure" has its usefulness mainly in carefully executed, small-sample studies; the "screening" procedure, *per contra*, has its usefulness mainly in reducing the size of the sample to manageable limits (as in the selection of potential delinquents for special study of experimental treatement).

One important characteristic of the Armed Forces' research was the scope of the studies undertaken. Thus, the number of cases included in the study was frequently quite large (by ordinary standards of educational research); the number and variety of measurements taken was also frequently large; the extent of statistical analysis was usually considerable; and the follow-through of "leads" or new hypotheses was, in some instances, quite thorough and persistent. Aimed at grand problems, some of the research was on a grand scale, and inevitably required a grand expenditure. In educational research, as elsewhere, methodology is related to the funds available.

Research conducted on a grand scale generally enjoys certain advantages, both scientific and financial. Even when immediately utiiitarian purposes predominate, it is virtually impossible thoughtfully to carry out an extensive, large-scale research without observing the potential value of methodogical improvements and theoretical advances. In small-scale research, the funds required to work on methodological and theoretical issues are rarely available; in large-scale research, it requires no more than a small fraction of the total funds to pursue such work, with potential returns so great that the possibilities are almost certain to be exploited, at least in part. The large-scale research enterprise can afford, also, to engage the services of top-flight directors and consultants. It is unfortunate that these advantages are rarely realized in peacetime educational research.

Conducting large research enterprises which required the expenditure of large funds, it was natural that the Armed Forces should organize research formally. There was, in fact, relatively little of the independent, personal research that characterizes most educational investigation in colleges and universities in peacetime. A hierarchy of control was set up in each of the armed services; and a broadly coordinating body, the Office of Scientific Research and Development, was established to exert over-all influence or control, particularly with regard to research contracts let to civilian agencies. No comparable coordinating body exists in educational research today. To what extent the absence of such a body represents a weak link in the methodology of educational research may be debatable; in the writer's opinion, additional coordination appears desirable—provided that coordination does not throttle intellectual independence and initiative. In the complexities of the social sciences, complete coordination of research would require omniscience, and should never be attempted.

One usual accompaniment of formal organization, whether of research or of operations, is a more-or-less systematic accounting of funds. Much of the research in education at the present time is conducted by college professors and students whose time and effort are not specifically charged (in an accounting sense) to research ; for all practical purposes, the cost of such educational research is hidden or only very approximately known.

The accounting of wartime research costs in the Armed Forces was more explicit and less approximate. Whether more accurate information on costs is a desirable aspect of over-all methodology in educational research today probably depends on circumstances. The absence of reasonably accurate accounting may connote a merely incidental or subsidiary status for research.

The Armed Forces' wartime research was, in the main, practical in nature, rather than "pure," "basic," or theory-oriented. This, however, is also true of much of the current research in civilian education todoy. A difference rests in this, that whereas the Armed Forces in general were ready and quick to make practical application of the research findings, the schools and colleges encounter numerous pressures opposed to the application of new research findings. Ideally, perhaps, the likelihood of reasonably quick application to current practice should be 'built into' research conducted for utilitarian purposes.

This, of course, is not easy to accomplish. It may require some sense of participation in the research by those ultimately cencerned (teachers, principals, superintendents, publicist, parents, school boards, etc.); or, at least, some orientation as to the nature and progress of the research. That such comparatively simple communication, however, should prove sufficient to insure the, prompt application of research seems highly dubious. How research methodogy (and procedures supplemental to research) can help to hasten appropriate application of research is itself one of the main problems confronting educational research today.

At several points in this presentation, it has been suggested or implied that too little transfer has been effected from Armed Forces' methodology to educational research. The causes for this inadequate transfer are moot. Perhaps civilian-minded researchers have been too ready to forget or overlook military experience.

More likely, the traditional dispersion of civilian educational research among numerous small units has worked against needed organizational developments. Certainly, difficulties in obtaining unrestricted funds constitute a handicapping factor. Finally, one may ask if educational research methodology has had its full measure of energetic, ingenious leadership, backed by high-level administrative support.

Whatever the causes, educational research methodology, interpreted in a broad sense, has not (in the writer's judgment) advanced as rapidly and profoundly as one could wish. Almost, it seems, a small-proprietorship system has continued where large-scale enterprise is needed. Granted that small units, like shops, enjoy certain unique advantages, it is also true that they suffer many limitations. Some super-market changes in educational research methodology appear overdue.

The account given above has at numerous points been couched in the past tense, because the amount of research conducted in the Armed Forces today which is relevant to education has dropped sharply. But some research is still going on, and most of the methodological characteristics of Armed Forces research mentioned above still prevail.

III. CONTRIBUTIONS THROUGH THE COOPERATIVE RESEARCH PROGRAME

Public Law 531, approved July 26, 1954, authorizes the U.S. Office of Education "to enter into contracts or jointly financed cooperative arrangements with universities and colleges and State educational agencies for the conduct of research, surveys, and demonstrations in the field of education." It is under this authorization, supported by annual appropriations from Congress, that the Cooperative Research Program of the Office of Education is conducted. The starting point in the program consists of the outline of a proposed project, submitted by the applicat ; added to this outline is a statement of the applicant's proposed financial contribution to the "jointly financed" study. Upon receipt by the Office of Education, the proposal is referred to one or more experts (either within or outside the Office of Education) for a confidential appraisal. These appraisals are then transmitted, along with the applicant's proposal, for review and study by a Research Advisory Committee composed of nationally recognized authorities in the field of educational research. The members of the Research Advisory Committee, meeting in Washington, discuss and evaluate the proposals, using an established set of criteria organized under four main headings; viz.,

(1) Significance of the Problem for Education;

(2) Soundness of the Research Design;

(3) Personnel and Facilities Available, and

(4) Economic Efficiency. or Relationship of Procedure and Probable Outcomes to Expenditure.

For each project, a recommendation of approval or disapproval is made by the committee to the Commissioner of Education. Of course, the number of projects favorably acted upon is limited by the funds available (the appropriation voted by Congress for the fiscall year 1959-60 was $ 3.2 million). For projects approved by the Commissioner, a contract is signed between the applicant and the United States; and the authorized funds are then made available as needed.

Such, rather briefly and elliptically, is the procedure for the receipt, appraisal, approval, and financial support of studies in the Cooperative Research Program. What are the effects of this program on the methodology of educational research ? Since no formal, 'ad boc,' quantitative study of this question has been made, the answer which follows must be impressionistic and logical, rather than objective and authoritative. Because the program has been well received and has, beyond question, stimulated or supported some excellent research, it seems fair to catalogue some of the favorable methodological effect first :

1. The programe has lifted the curse of insufficient funds with all the inadequacies of scope, staffing, and techniques which this implies—from the studies it supports.

2. The program has encouraged and supported larger, and consequently more meaningful and more adequate, research projects than would otherwise have been undertaken. The importance of this gain is difficult to overemphasize. In a field as complicated and ramified as education, the methodology or strategy of small studies and bit-by-bit progress is inefficient. Small studies, of course, have their value

—especially for purposes of exploration in expensive domains, or where essential techniques have not yet been well developed. But small studies arising merely from lack of funds, rather than from considerations of suitability, have long been more common than useful.

3. The criteria adhered to by the Research Advisory Committee have led to higher quality and standards of research design and statistical analysis. As yet, of course, this effect is limited to studies supported by the program. The models provided by such studies however, exert a broad, significant influence on other studies, outside the programe.

4. The organization and staffing of projects have been improved. Provision is made, in every case, for a project director, usually supported by as many consultants as the special features or difficulties of the project require; encouragement is given, too, to the employment of promising graduate students or recent Ph. D.'s 'with full compensation'. The expectation is that these young persons, receiving additional experience and training in research, may be led to a full-time career in educational research, or, at least, to a greater concentration on research than would otherwise be likely.

5. The selection procedure which is employed in the choice of projects for program support—namely, the use of confidential expert appraisal, followed by general evaluation by a well-qualified panel—is itself a noteworthy aspect of methodology. This procedure, widely used by Federal agencies for the choice of research projects, has scientific as well as administrative advantages. (Possible disadvantages of the procedure will be considered at a later point)

6. Finally, the method of 'joint financing' of research projects by the Government and the applicant institu-

tion appears to have several significant advantages. From the point of view of the Government, the joint financing helps to assure prudent management in the use of funds by the institution; and thus to generate the confidence which is essential if continued appropriations are to be expected from Congress. From the point of view of the institution, the joint financing helps to sustain the scientific independence of the institution—both in the selection of research problems and the proposed techniques to be employed. The maintenance of the scientifice independence or integrity of those engaged in educational research is clearly an essential requirement of any sound scientific methodology.

The posive effects noted above are eagerly sought by all persons connected with the Cooperative Research Program; and it is reasonable to suppose that they are, at least in some measure, actually achieved. There is, of course, an opposite side of the ledger, where possible negative effects require recognition. Such effects, while as eagerly fought as the positive effects are sought, may still not be wholly avoidable.

1. The Cooperative Research Program, like most government-sponsored research programs, is conducted through individual 'projects.' The support of projects may be contrasted with the support of broad 'programs' of research, or—allowing still greater freedom and imposing virtually no restrictions or controls— with 'unrestricted institutional grants' for uncommitted (or only very broadly identified) research goals. Concerning these three approaches, the President's Advisory Committee has written :

> Unfortunately there is a tendency to believe that in providing a contract or grant for a single specific project the chance of finding a solution to a problem is being maximized and is also more economical. In reality, however, the overall research effort may be hurt. Program grants or institutional grants would permit more effective research in broad areas of science and provide greater freedom

for the scientific community to give direction to the work undertaken. They might also prove to be an important adiministrative device for reducing the potential growth of Government adiministration if, otherwise, a greatly increased number of seclecting and reviewing boards were necessary.

In passing, it must be observed that the adoption of a policy of program and institutional grants would require much larger funds than are currently available to the Cooperative Research Program.

2. Legal counsel of the Department of Health, Education, and Welfare has advised that the Cooperative Research Program must operate through 'contracts' not 'grants'. The principal distinction is that, under a contract, the means to be employed by the investigator in fulfilling the purpose of his research, and timing of his work, are more particularly spelled out than under a grant. Thus, the investigator under a contract has less freedom or flexibility to alter his procedures, as unforeseen difficulties or opportunities present themselves; on the other hand, it may be that, in the development of a contract, sufficient forethought is exercised so that alterations become less frequently needed. Freedom and flexibility are, of course, precious assets of scientific procedure or methodology; from this point of view, the superiority of grants is important. This superiority is blunted, however, by two factors :

(1) It is possible, within the framework of a contract to formulate an agreement which allows the investigator reasonable leeway—although the degree of freedom thus allowed will generally not be as great as under the terms of a grant; and

(2) Provision can be made for amendment of the contract, provided that such amendment is "in the interest of the Government." In the writer's observation and interpretation, these two factors successfully mitigate, though they do not eliminate, the rigidity of the contractual form.

3. The Cooperative Research Program was authorized by Congress and depends on Congress for annual appropriations. Does this lead to any bending or adaptation by investigators to the supposed preferences of Congress ? Does it lead to the intrusion of Congressional influence in the selection of projects by the Research Advisory Committee or the Commissioner of Education ?

In the writer's observation and interpretation, the answer to the second question is an emphatic 'no'. With regard to the first question, it is 'possible' that Congressional interest and the dependence on annual Congressional appropriations may, in the area of educational research, lead to an undue emphasis on practical or applied, rather than theory-oriented, studies; and it is 'possible' that undue preference may be given to proposals which make use of objective or "understandable" techniques, rather than procedures which are more esoteric or less obvious.

These possibilities are somewhat difficult to assess. Certainly the political influence, if any, appears minimal up to the present. Even a slight curtailment of scientific freedom by political process, however, should be viewed seriously, both by the scientific and by the politician. It is safe to say that Congressmen, in the main,are sincere in their wish to support research and are read to defer to the requirements of scientific methodology. The ultimate hope of science in this domain would appear to lie in an educated, alert, electorate, kept informed by an energetic, public-spirited, free press (including radio and TV). In this connection, it mighl prove useful to evaluate the comparative freedom of educational research under Federal vs. private auspices; we are not convinced that the advantage would always lie with the private arrangement.

4. At the heart of the Cooperative Research Program is the Research Advisory Committee, which (subject only to approval by the Commissioner of Education) is responsible for selection of the proposals to be accorded financial support. Whether justly or otherwise, committees are generally reputed to be "conservative," i.e., to be somewhat unsympathetic or

unreceptive to the unconventional, the exceptional, of the different—in a word, to "play it safe." The President's Science Advisory Committee (itself a committee !) has expressed it thus :

> Inevitably, the principal seclecting agencies in Government are bound to be influenced to some degree by advisers who are moved by intellectual styles of the time. including such things as scholarly "success" of work already done in the field. The climate and the means should be created whereby ideas which are challenging and sound but unconventional and different can be hospitably considered and encouraged.

If a selection committee leans toward the conventionally conceived and comparatively "safe" proposal, we may expect to see some bias in favor of, say, the experimental and objective studies, rather than the theoretical, reflective, or subjective; toward studies involving controlled situations, rather than those involving uncontrolled or more natural situations; toward the short, quick study, rather than the long drawn-out one; toward the low-cost study, rather than the high-cost; toward the study with the added appeal of practical application, rather than the one oriented toward (say) techniques of measurement, problems of methodology, or uncertain exploration.

If this is so, the effects must be unfortunate; for no element is more crucial or basic to sound scientific methodology than the 'intellectual freedom' of the investigator in his choice of problems and procedures. Conservatism of the type hypothesized above would produce studies leading to proof or confirmation, rather than discovery; to development, rather than exploration; to gradual progress, rather than innovation and possible "break-through."

The saving feature, in all this, is that any advisory committee of national stature is alert to the dangers of conservatism or over-caution in the selection of projects. Of course, a committee responsible for the distribution of limited public funds will rarely support extremely individualistic or speculative projects. Nor should it. Such projects, if considered worth the risk, should receive consideration and support from other sources, such as foundations, universities, or corporations. Thus the very existence of public support for research, as in the Cooperative Research Program, makes it "vitally important...... that the Government's science policy does not discourage private support of science, and indeed, that it takes pains to encourage more of it."

5. Public Law 531 is concerned with research, but does not mention the dissemination of research findings. One tenable view is that research without dissemination is incomplete and, indeed, pointless. On this view, dissemination is quintessential, and should be "built into" any valid research methodology. The Cooperative Research Program, following Public Law 531, does not place responsibility on its contractors to do this; but those in charge of the program are keenly aware of the imporatnce of making the results of research known, and are taking significant steps to assure more adequate dissemination than would otherwise occur.

Educational research receives financial support from the Office of Education not only through the Cooperative Research Program under Public Law 531 but also through other units of the office under the National Defense Education Act of 1958 (Title VI, "Language Development," and Title VII, "Research and Experimentation in More Effective Utilization of Televison, Radio, Motion Pictures, and Releted Media for Educational Purposes"). It is too early, yet, to assess the effects of this additional financial support on educational research methodology. Three other Federal agencies which occasionally give financial support to educational research include the National Institute of Mental Health, the Office of Vocational Rehabilitation (both within the Department of Health, Education, and Welfare,) and the National Science Foundation.

IV. CLOSING REMARKS

In this discussion the phrase "educational research methodology" has been given a broad interpretation, extending beyoud specifically technical aspects (as in the development of a survey) to factors which affect the choice of a problem, the conduct of the research, and the utilization of findings. The Federal contributions to educational research methodology discussed in Part I above ("Contributions through National Surveys") are principally technical, in Part II ("Contributions through Research in the Armed Forces"), are technical, financial and organizational, and in Part III ("Contributions through the Cooperative Research Program"), are financial, organizational, and—for want of a better term— governmental.

If there is any central thesis in the present paper, it is that the indispensable, vital core of any sound scientific methodology is intellectual freedom. Also of paramount significance are adequate financing and proper organization and staffiing. Essential to the successful functioniny of these factors is a social framework which places a high value on truth and its discovery. In none of these basic elements have the contributions of the Federal government led to anything approaching perfection. But progress is being made; and the burden of this paper is that the Federal contribution to such progress has been substantial.

survey) to factors which affect the choice of a problem, the conduct of the research, and the utilization of findings. The Federal contributions to educational research methodology discussed in Part I above ("Contributions through National Surveys") are principally technical, in Part II ("Contributions through Research in the Armed Forces"), are technical, financial and organizational, and in Part III ("Contributions through the Cooperative Research Program"), are financial, organizational, and—for want of a better term—governmental.

If there is any central thesis in the present paper, it is that the indispensable, vital core of any sound scientific methodology is intellectual freedom. Also of paramount significance are adequate financing and proper organization and staffing. Essential to the successful functioning of these factors is a social framework which places a high value on truth and its discovery. In none of these basic elements have the contributions of the Federal government led to anything approaching perfection. But progress is being made, and the burden of this paper is that the Federal contribution to such progress has been substantial.

9

Behavioral Sciences and Educational Research

RALPH W. TYLER
Center for Advanced Study in the Behavioral Sciences

This topic is very broad, both because of the range of the disciplines included in the behavioral sciences and because of the variety of fields incompassed in the total of educational research. The study of human behavior includes biological studies such as neurophysiology, genetics, psychiatry, human ecology; social studies such as anthropology, economics, history, political science, psychology, sociology; and some scientific studies of behavior in humanistic fields, particularly by certain students of philosophy and literature. Educational research includes studies of the curriculum, of instruction and pupil learning, of guidance and counseling, of teaching personnel, of buildings and physical facilities, of organization, administration, and supervision. An attempt to review the contributions of all the behavioral sciences to all fields of educational research would be superficial both because of time limitations and because of the limitations of my own competence. What I shall do is to identify the contributions with which I am familiar and which seem to me to have future as well as present value for the improvement of educational research.

Since my own interests have largely been in the field of curriculum and instruction, the contributions of the behavioral sciences which I can identify largely relate to this field. However, I hope that they will also serve as illustrations which can be extended to other studies in the behavioral sciences, and to other fields of educational research.

I. KINDS OF CONTRIBUTIONS

Do not expect the behavioral sciences to provide direct answers to the basic questions posed for educational research. Since education is a purposeful enterprise conducted to accomplish certain social and personal ends, the basic questions which educational research seeks to answer or to help answer are questions such as these.

What are the proper objectives of a school or college or some other educational institution or program ?

What kinds of educational experiences can be provided which will achieve these objectives ?

How can these experiences be organized to maximize their educational effectiveness ?

How can the effectiveness of educational programs be appraised ?

Who should be educated in a particular institution or program and how should they be selected and guided ?

What kinds of educational personnel are required and how should they be selected and educated ?

What administrative organizations, policies, and procedures are effective in conducting educational institutions and programs ?

What facilities are needed ?

How can educational institutions and programs be effectively supported ?

The behaviorial sciences, on the other hand, are not asking questions about what should be done or how a task can be effectively accomplished. The behavioral sciences look at behavioral phenomena as natural processes and seek to explain what is going on, what factors are involved, what relations there are among these factors and, so far as possible, what antecedent events commonly lead to what subsequent events. Thus, a behavioral scientist may be trying to explain how a given kind of learning takes place, rather than to decide what should be learned or how it can be taught. Or the behavioral scientist may be trying to find out the way in which community pressure groups operate rather than how to gain support for the public school.

Because of this difference in the kinds of questions under study, the behavioral sciences not only may fail to provide direct answers to the questions of primary concern to edcational research but they may also contribue less in the natuie of research findings than they do to the development of conceptualizations useful in planning and interpreting studies of education and to the invention of techniques for designing studies, and for collecting and analyzing the data of educational research.

Education is an integral part of modern life. Modern individual and social life encompasses a great complexity of phenomena. Systematic and orderly investigations of the "great buzzing confusion" of life require conceptualizations, that is, views of what to look for, how to look for them, and what kinds of structures, processes, and relationships are involved. If when one entered a classroom he had no prior conceptualization of teaching and learning, he would see children and an adult, he would hear several children and the adult speaking. he would note physical items in the room, movements of people, and the like. What gives it meaning for the investigator of classroom instruction is a "model" which he conceives, a simplified picture of the structure and process of classroom instruction.

This model usually includes such elements as a teacher, pupils, objectives of instruction, methods of teaching, materials of instruction, learning outcomes. If he holds such a model in mind, he has a basis for focusing his observations and for arranging and analyzing his data.

This development of a formal model provides a way of viewing the complex phenomena in a fashion which permits scientific study. Models serve to simplify a process which appears on the surface to be too voried or complex or haphazard to be understood. But models must not only simplify complex phenomena but they must provide a means for explaining and predicting the variations and regularities observed in the phenomena. Hence, conceptualizations change a research indicates that earlier models fail to explain or predict many of the observations noted. For example, a common model for research in instruction in the 1920's included a teacher, a group of pupils, methods of teaching, learning outcomes.

This conceptualization recognized variations in the intelligence of pupils, various methods of teaching and variations in the degree of achievement by the pupils of the learning outcomes. Since that time, a number of things have been added to this model, such as variations in the skills, preparation, and personalities of teachers, variations in the initial achievement of pupils, in the kinds of pupil motivation, in the content and intensity of pupil interests, and variations among several major kinds of educational outcomes, such as knowledge, skills. attitudes, and problem-solving. Effective educational research is commonly guided by conceptualizations which provide ways of viewing the complexity of educational phenomena in orderly and meaningful patterns. Later on in this paper illustrations are presented of contributions the behavioral sciences are making to our conceptualizations of educational phenomena.

Research in education also requires techniques for designing studies and for collecting and analyzing data. Mathematical statistics and experimental work in some of the biological sciences have provided many of the current techniques used in designing experiments and in selecting sample populations. The behavioral sciences have also contributed here. Even more frequently have the behavioral sciences developed methods for collecting and analyzing data which are being used in educational research. In general, as the illustrations in the following sections indicate, the contributions of the behavioral sciences to educational research are chiefly in providing useful concepts and techniques rather than in furnishing answers to educational questions.

II. ILLUSTRATIONS FROM ANTHROPOLOGY

The early work of social anthropologists involved the study of primitive societies, and in recent years their efforts have extended to the study of modern communities. Each of these societies has developed patterns of life which are in some respects unique. The pattern of acceptable behavior in a givens society is commonly called its culture. It includes certain value, which are preferred to others, certain attitudes which characterize its members, certain language patterns, certain ways of getting things done. To survive in a culture and to take a responsible place in it require the transmission to each new generation of the basic values, attitudes, skills, practices, and the like.

This is a process which begins in the early days of infancy and, in many cases, parents and other adults may be quite unconscious of the task in which they are engaged. In more complex societies, specialized institutions, schools, are responsible for part of the process of inducting young people into the culture. Also, anthropologists note that in most complex societies each city includes not one culture but several groups, each with its own culture, groups which may be held together by common nationality origins or common religious faiths or common socio-economic status.

The relevance of these studies to the planning and conduct of educational research has become obvious. Our conceptualization of education must be comprehensive enough to include the wide range of learning involved in acculturation. In becoming an adult, a child is acquiring values, attitudes, knowledge, skills, habits, not only those given attention in the schools but those that are important in his culture.

Furthermore, the culture in which he lives may be different from the culture of another child in the same schoolroom, and it may be different from the culture in which the teacher lives. This means that our model for research will often need to include categories to define the relevant features of the cultures or sub-cultures of the various pupils and teachers involved.

At times it will need to take into account the similarity or dissimilarity between the objectives of the school and its practices and the objectives of acculturation and the common practices in the pupil's culture. Where the purposes of the school are unrelated to, or in conflict with, the values of the pupil's culture, or where the ways of life in the school are in conflict with the practices in his culture, the educational results are likely to be very different from those obtained with pupils whose culture patterns are similar to the objectives and practice of the school.

Anthropology is not only contributing concepts of this type to aid our thinking about education, but its methods of investigation have provided us with tools useful in educational research. Two of these come readily to mind - the use of informants and participant observation. In the use of informants, persons who are central subjects of investigation are queried at length ond at several times to gain from them reports on how the society operates as they see it. Seeing a culture through the eyes of its members in this way throws light on values and attitudes which are not commonly apparent to the outsider. Hence, studies of pupil groups, of teacher groups, of pressure groups and the like, are increasingly making use of informants.

Similarly, participant observation is a method of data collection which seeks to get inside the culture. More detailed information and greater accuracy are sought by having research workers themselves become part of the culture under investigation. This method is being used in studies of college and professional students and of teaching personnel,

III. ILLUSTRATIONS FROM SOCIAL PSYCHOLOGY

Social psychologists are helping to clarify the significance of social groups in their relation to individual human behavior. Man is born into a family, all of his earliest potent experiences involve at least one other person, usually the mother. With the children of his own family, or in the neighborhood, much of his early exploration outside the home takes place. The school, the church, the playground, the working situation, to enumerate only a few, are all contexts in which life is lived, and they are group contexts. Groups, particularly the small, face-to-face groups, are shown to influence individual behavior profoundly, as the individual at the same time is influencing the group.

Studies have shown that most groups attend both to the recognized purpose for which they exist and also to the emotionalized social relations within the group. Where the group social relations are under tension, where the individuals are uncertain or unhappy about their status in the group, there is little progress by the group in attaining its recognized purpose. Where group relations are stable and the individuals are clear about their status and find it acceptable, the group morale is high ; it is in fine condition for pursuing its basic purposes.

The studies also suggest that it is in the various small groups of which an individual is a member that the greatest development and modification of behavior takes place. Purely formal membership in school, or church, or political party, or labor union, or other organization usually means little compared to the influence of the family, the gang, the friendship group, the small "outfit" with whom he works, and the like. These groups provide the milieu in which significant changes in attitudes, habits, and practices may take place.

The social psychologists' work on small groups has noticeably influenced educational research. Increasingly, studies of personality development in children and youth in school and college and studies of successes and failures in educational achievement are analyzing the peer groups to which the pupils belong, noting that some peer groups provide reinforcement for the learning emphasized by the school, that other peer groups may insulate their members from school influences, that still other peer groups may operate to teach values and practices in opposition to the school objectives.

Furthermore, some research in classroom instruction has involved experimentation with small groups as units for teaching and learning. A class of thirty or forty may be reconstituted into several groups of from three to eight members, each group assuming responsibilities which require group planning, group attack, group review and appraisal, group discipline, and group rewards. It is hypothesized that such learning experiences will have great influence if each group becomes well-integrated and concentrates its attention on the jab at hand.

Social psychologists are also suggesting the importance of perception as a factor in behavior, particularly in learning. How one reacts to a given situation is largely determined by what he sees in that situation. Furthermore, one's attitudes are, in considerable measure, shaped by his perception. How he feels about persons, objects, or events is greatly influenced by what he sees in them, and several persons looking at the same phenomena will often see different things. Present evidence indicates that one's perception of objects, persons, or events takes shape in the early contact with them and remains fairly stable in spite of many later opportunities to check the inadequacies of the early perception.

The early perception is often formed by the suggestions of others as well as by one's own careful observation. Thus, children may early develop the notion that the sea is blue, partly perhaps from observing it when it was blue and partly by the suggestions of others, as in paintings. It is found the most children continue to "see" a blue sea even when asked to observe it when it is clearly gray or brown or green.

Or, to cite another example, children may at an early age develop the notion of a butcher as a fat, jolly man. This perception often continues to operate even when children are asked to observe butchers who are, to an objective observer, lean and dour. Perception of both physical and social phenomena is quite likely to be stereotyped in spite of many opprtunities for correcting the inadequacies of earlier perceptions. Since one's behavior is strongly influenced by what one sees in the situation, and since much of what one "sees" is the memory of an earlier perception, reaction to situations are often unrealistic because one's perception is unrealistic.

The importance of this concept of subjective perception for the planning, conduct, and interpretation of educational research is only currently becoming recognized, Frequently, studies of curriculum and instruction will need to include data on the perceptions of pupils regarding the objects of study, the learning task, the teacher, and other pupils, as well as perceptions of the teachers regarding their purposes and their pupils, Studies of guidance may also need to include data on how the pupil is perceived by other pupils, by teachers, and by guidance counselors ; how the guidance counselor perceives his task ; and how the pupil perceives the activity and the persons involved in it. Studies of administration and of teaching personnel will also find this concept helpful.

Social psychologists have also developed techniques useful in callecting and analyzing data, such as the sociogram for identifying status relations, cliques, and influence networks within peer groups ; the one-way vision room for studying small group behavior ; the adjective check list and semantic differential for describing and measuring perception ; the controlled experiment for testing social influences on perception. These are becoming common instruments used by educational research workers.

IV. ILLUSTRATIONS FROM PERSONALITY STUDIES

Psychiatrists and personality psychologists have focused attention on the sequences of development through which the individual moves as the passes from early childhood to mature adulthood. As the individual's anatomical and physiological system grows and matures and as he encounters the demands and expectations of the society in which he lives, he is faced with a series of developmental challenges which he commonly tries to meet. In the first two years of life, for example, he is expected to gain control over his physical body so that he can walk, talk, eat, use the toilet, and the like. In adolescence, he is confronted with the challenge of achieving an autonomous self, independent from close parental controls.

Although there are some variations in the lists of developmental tasks prepared by different researchers, the concept is quite generally used in the personality field. Its significance for educational research lies in its relation to the motivation and direction of attention of students in schools and colleges.

A high school girl preoccupied with the developmental task of relating effectively to age mates of the opposite sex may devote her major energies and attention to this task while failing to engage productively in the educational activities planned by the school. A college freshman who is encountering difficulty in achieving independence from the family may throw his major efforts into college activities which are controlled by students to gain independent recognition. The educational research worker is often required to build a model which makes explicit the several driving purposes of students and the various areas of life in which these purposes may be worked out. Then, the educational program can be understood in this perspective.

From the personality field also come the concepts of needs and press. Human beings have basic personality needs such as the need to belong to a social group, the need for status or respect, the need for affection. The environment, particularly the social environment, exerts a certain press upon the individual which the individual views as a demand or expectation for certain characteristics, such as the press for independence in the case of some environments, the press for dependence in others. Where the individual's needs and the press of his environment are congruent, stable personality development is expected, while lack of congruence may lead to tension and conflicts.

These concepts suggest to educational research workers a model for study of the educational effects of a school or college in which the students are described or measured in terms of their personality needs, while the school or college is described or measured in terms of the environmental press characteristic of it, that is, the demands and expectations commonly communicated to students. Presumably, remaining in school and doing well in school would be more frequently found with students whose personality needs were similar to the demands and expectations of the school. while more frequently drop outs and failures would be found with students whose personality needs were unrelated to or in conflict with the press of the school environment. These concepts are getting into the planning of educational research.

Another useful concept developed by students of personality is identification. Commonly, from early childhood on through adolescence a child or youih finds in his environment someone else, usually an older person, whom he greatly admires, and he takes this person as an ideal to be closely emulated. In this process of emulation the child frequently imagines himself to be the other person and in this sense he identifies with the ideal. In seeking to be like the other person the child takes on the values and attitudes of his ideal insofar as the child can perceive them. He also attempts to develop the skills and follow the habits and practices of his ideal as he perceives them. In terms of this conception, identification is one of the major means by which children and youth acquire new values and attitudes and develop new habits and practices.

Normally, as a child grows up he finds a succession of ideas with whom he identifies—parent, teacher, youth leader, upper-classman, athlete, gangster, doctor—persons who seem to him to be interesting, rewarding, attractive, prestigeful, and at the same time seem to be within his power of attainment. The nature of these ideals, the values they demonstrate, the attitudes they reflect, the type of life they portray are of great importance in influencing the development of the child and youth.

This concept of identification is relevant at several points in developing models to guide educational research. In studying school learning, particularly motivation, and the achievement of objectives in the areas of values, attitudes, habits and practices, explanations for the results observed may often require a study of the identification process in the school groups who are the subjects of investigation.

Who are the attractive persons in the environment of these children ?

With whom do the children identify ?

How do the children perceive the values, attitudes, habits, and practices of these ideals ?

The extension of the research in these directions may often serve to provide a more adequate understanding of the findings. Furthermore, research concerned with the selection, assignment, and effectiveness of teaching personnel may, at times, be aided by using this concept of identification in planning and interpeting studies.

Do children identify with this teacher ?

What ages and types of children ?

How is this teacher perceived by these children ?

That is, what values, attitudes, habits, and practices do these children attribute to this teacher ?

From these data, what predictions may be made regarding the kinds of children who will be markedly influenced by this teacher ?

What will be the nature of these influences ?

Answers to these questions may help to develop a more comprehensive and valid theory regarding bases for selecting, assigning, and guiding the professional growth of teachers.

From personality psychology and psychiatry have come two useful techniques for collecting data that are now frequently employed by educational research workers, the projective test and the depth interview. Projective tests such as the TAT, the Rorschach, and the sentence completion present to the subject an ambiguous situation relating to an area of personal involvement and ask the subject to clarify the situation. Since the situation is ambiguous, whatever the subject puts into it to explain it must come from his own interpretation. Hence, the projective test may serve to bring to the surface attitudes, perceptions, and similar reactions which are commonly unrevealed. It may help to identify personality needs, conflicting attitudes, interests and values, and distorted perceptions. Probably the projective test most frequently used in educational research is the TAT, or Thematic Apperception Test. This consists of a series of pictures which present situations like the relations between parent and child in a setting which is ambiguous. The child is asked to tell what is happening in the picture. His explanation may indicate his own perception of parents and of parent-child relationships. In this way data may be obtained which cannot be got from direct observation or questioning.

In similar fashion, the depth interview is a technique for getting information about attitudes and values that are commonly below the surface. The depth interview is indirect, open-ended, permissive, broadly and vaguely focused, and may often use third persons as subjects of discussion rather than the thoughts, feelings, or actions of the principals. Because it is very time-consumings and because it requires considerable skill to interpret, the depth interview has been less frequently used in educational research than the projective test.

V. ILLUSTRATIONS FROM SOCIOLOGY

Probably the most widely used sociological concept in educational research is that of social stratification. Every society of large-scale sociall organization is conceived to be composed of several social classes, that is, collections of people of a similar level of social prestige and public respect. These several strata of society are commonly found in each town and city, with the social classes corresponding roughly to income and occupational levels. From the standpoint of their influence on human behavior, there are two major characteristics of this social class structure:

(a) Each social class sets a pattern of conventional or acceptable behavior for its members, and

(b) the hierarchy of social classes in terms of social prestige or public respect forms a ladder to direct the actions of members of a lower social class who seek to rise in public esteem and social recognition.

The pattern of acceptable behavior in one social class differs in various respects from that of another. Among children of lower classes, fighting is an approved form of behavior. The use of certain four-letter words is acceptable in some classes and not in others. Sharp differences in etiquette, dress, table manners, and the like are noticeable. Many parents in lower-middle classes desire higher prestige for their children. They often find cues for educating children for uppper-middle class roles by observing the models of middle class behavior shown in movies, television, radio, magazines, newspapers, and the like. Thus, the hierarchy of social classes exerts a powerful directive influence on those who seek to climb the social ladder.

Social stratification is a concept that has already had considerable influence upon educational research. For example, the past fifteen years have witnessed the inclusion of social class as a major variable or category of analysis in studies involving school children, teachers, and communities. The concept has made us conscious of the inadequacy of some of our previous notions about the educability of particular individuals and groups of children. The vocabulary, the kinds of problems used, and the accepted behaviour of the schools reflcet the middle class, old American culture. Children who come from other groups employing different vocabularies, accustomed to different types of problems and being rewarded or punished for different partterns of behavior find the typical classroom confusing and the classroom activities difficult to carry on. They are ofen-udged to be mediocre or slow learners and are frequently advised to attempt only the required minimum of formal schooling. Yet studies of problem-solving among various social classes indicate a considerable number of children and youth in every class who are adept in attacking problems when the problems are real to them and couched in their language.

So there is an increasing interest in identifying kinds of learning experiences which are meaningful to pupils from lower social classes and which can help to increrse the effectiveness of the schools in woring with these children. There is also interest in devising tests that may serve as better indicators of the educability of lower class children than do the current tests of scholastic aptitude which largely include middle class vocabulary and problems.

Involved in the concept of social stratification is that of social mobility. In stratified social organizations are a number of individuals who are strongly motivated to climb the social ladder and to move into social classes which have greater prestige or public esteem. Those who are able to move from one social class to another are conceived to be socially mobile. In American society social mobility is considerably greater than is characteristic of the older European or Asian societies. Education is one of the chief means for social mobility. By the aid of education, children of unskilled and skilled laborers have frequently become middle class civil servants, teachers, manager, and the like. On ther hand, some who greatly desire to move up the social ladder do not do so. The study of the socially mobile in comparison with those who are not mobile indicates differences in ability and in personality characteristics. Such studies also suggest some of the costs of high social mobility to the individual, such as a feeling of loneliness and rootlessness, conflicts in values and loyalties, and loss of direction when maximum social elevation has been reached.

Social mobility is a useful concept to include in the models used to guide research relating to motivation of learning and rewards in learning. It is also helpful in planning studies of teaching and administrative personnel in schools, because teachers and school administrators include within their ranks persons who differ greatly in their social mobility and it can be hypthesized that their behavior and their careers will also differ.

The concept of social institutions is another contribution of sociology. The family, the school, the church, the factory are examples of common social institutions. Each social institution can be viewed in terms of its functions, its its structure, the roles that are to be performed by the peoples in the institution, and the communication channels, both formal and informal, through which attitudes and actions are directed. This way of conceptualizing the school for study has been most useful in research concerned with administration, but it has had some value in studies of curriculum and instruction. It has been shown that the pupils' notions of the proper roles of the proper roles of the teacher influence the responses pupils make to instruction.

When the expectations of pupils about the teacher's role differ from that of the teacher himself, the learning is likely to be less than when there is congruence between the teacher's idea of his role and the idea that the pupils have of the proper role for the teacher. Furthermore, the identification of the two channels of communication found in typical social institutions; the discovery that these channels differ in their impact upon the members of the institution offer promise of adding a factor which may help further to explain student attitudes, student morale, and student-faculty relations.

Among the contributions sociology is making to the techniques of educational research, probably the sample survey is most widely used. The early tradition in educational research emphasized tests, written questionnaires, official records. The possibilities of personal interviews applied to a large population of pupils, teabhers, parents, and other community members were demonstrated by the public opinion polls and the more sophisticated sample surveys. Now these methods are increasingly used in various fields of educational research. The construction of interview schedulds, the selection of representative samples of given populations, and the technique of interviewing have each become a highly refined and well-codified methodology with applications in many areas.

VI. OTHER FIELDS

The limitations of time preclude me from giving more illustrations. If more time were available I should like to suggest illustrations from economics, political science, and history in order to give a somewhat more varied picture of the kinds of contributions being made by the behavioral sciences. The construction of models for measuring economic growth and development suggests ways of estimating the economic contribution education is moking to our society, the analysis of our current dynamic economy is indicating two new functions for public education, and the concept of marginal utility is serving as a model for some of the current research on relative motivation in learning.

In political science, the development of information theory and the concept of the decision-making process as a basic unit in political behavior have possibilities for more adequately explaining teacher behavior and pupil group behavior. Political scientists have also elaborated the concept of pressure groups and have conceived of effective policy decisions as those which help to bring into equilibrium the conflicting pressures of these groups. Such concepts have obvious uses in studies of administration. History makes major contributions in such ways as the sophisticated concept of development over time, and in its methods of bringing to bear upon a given problem several different influences and events. These are but sketchy suggestions which cannot be amplified now. Since the intent of this presentation, however, is to illustrate, rather than to treat comprehensively, the kinds of contributions made by the behavioral sciences, the foregoing examples may be sufficient.

VII. CONCLUDING STATEMENT

The behavioral sciences have a different purpose from that of educational research, hence they cannot take the place of research studies focused on problems of education. Nevertheless, the behavioral sciences have been and will continue to make important contributions to educational research. In general, they are contributions to the conceptualization of the problems, contributions in the form of research techniques, and, to a lesser extent, contributions of useful findings. Although the behavioral sciences are not providing direct answers to important educational questions, they are proving of great assistance in the development of a soundly-based program of educational research.

10

Discussions on Educational Research

Discussion Following Paper Presented by Nicbolas Fattu

PIERCE: Are all professors interested in doing research ?

FATTU: No. In fact a minority of professors are interested. The percentages I have given here in the distribution of time are representative of the faculty. When you ask a dean to indicate how many of his professors do research and then compare that with the total group of faculty, you will find that it is very definitely a small minority. In other words, the individuals who are motivated to do research or toward research are not more, in some cases, than well, say one-fourth. If I were to give a figure, one-fourth of the total group. Let's not be misled by this figure. I think we can note differences in atmosphere.

Some of these people among the three-fourths who do not do research give the impression that they understand and utilize research in their teaching. Then there are others, and, I am sad to say, they seem to be in a majority, who give the impression that they are not particularly interested in research, that research is an activity you indulge in, but after all you have to get on with the main business of teaching, and research has settled so few problems that you have to use judgement, and materials that are already available, to attack these problems on a global scale.

LAMBERT : Were you able to assess the level of ability of people doing research? I'm not thinking primarily of the college dean or the full professor, but the person down the line who might be in a position of research assistant or graduate student, who possibly is carrying on the real work involved in a research design of some type. Do you have any reactions, or were you able to draw any conclusions of your own concerning the general level of quality of these people, that is, their general background, their education, whether they were outstanding people, whether they were fully based in research methodology, and so on ?

FATIU : We looked at some distributions of ability levels of graduate students and these distributions showed that at the upper end of the scale these students were just as high as any students in any school. But unfortunately this is a skewed distribution and we had a much larger proportion of the group towards the lower end of the scale than did the people in physics or the physical sciences and psychology. for example.

LAMBERT : I wonder if part of this problems is the fact that we expect to get educational research done for nothing ?

FATTU : Oh, there is no question that we try to get educational research done for nothing. All the data suggest that we don't give much attention to financial reward; in other words, educators like preachers work for love of the job and not for the financial reward. This, I would underscore, is especially true of educational research workers Now, it is not true in two institution. In two institution I noticed that the "research bureau" was concerned with consultative services, with studies of school planning and was to on and was to a large extent used as a means of supplementing faculty salaries, and other faculty members rather enviously told me that it very generously supplemented their salaries, so that it become the main focus of attention rather than the teaching.

CHERRY : I wonder if that statement you just made isn't the key to our whole difficulty, and it seems to me to be further reflected in the points you have made in connection with what is educational research and what do we seek our of educational research. Unless we get a better answer to this question, an answer that has more meaning to more of us than have been able to get so far, are we going to be able to orient ourselves and the people who support our activities so that we can carry on research ? This leaves me feeling a little low when I see the efforts made by these selected institutions to define what it is we are trying to do in educational research.

FATTU : My comment would be that to a certain extent it is wholesome not to define what is meant by educational research, except in a very general way. I think a classic example is the public health service, that is, the National Institute of Health projects with respect to mental illness. Ten years ago if we had said that studies ought to be concerned with behavioral research and the like, and that only this is what constitutes the study of mental health, we would have failed entirely to study chemotherapy. Today shock treatment and some other treatments that were used a decade ago are almost entirely out and the treatment of mental illness is largely on a chemical basis. One young man was even treating reading disabilities on a chemical basis and getting some very interesting abilities.

He had a very nice conceptual sceeme in which he worked out a physiology of why some kinds of readers who had been diagnosed as people with reading diffculties - individuals who did not respond to educative treatment – responded when these particular drugs were administered, I doubt if we will ever reach the stage when we will get a pill that will improve the learning ability of average students by a factor of five per cent or so. But this is a problem on which a lot of research has been done by psychologists. The fact that there has been one such study is most interesting. I don't know if I made myself clear, but this is the point that I want to make: If we rely. not upon the definition of the field, but upon the preparation of the people who do research and upon the setting of, let us say, standards for research to meet, I think we are doing much more constructive work than if we tried to describe and circumscribe what is educational research.

CHERRY : I would agree, I think we need to give a great deal more consideration to this problem than we have done in the past.

FATIU : Oh, I agree with you, I would say the comment is more appropriate and it summarizes what the case actually is. We have not defined what the field of educational research is, but, in my judgment, I think we would be wasting time if we spent a lot of effort in defining educational research, beyond the point of getting at the business of studying phenomena which are concerned with the educative process and relevant factors.

BANGHART : I am not sure that this question is quite relevant; perhaps you have covered it. I don't get a very vivid sense of the kind of problems that are demanding solution. That is, you mentioned the fact that perhaps educational research is something that people expect to get for nothing. On the other hand, in many areas where active research is certainly going on there is a large class of problems demanding solution. Would you care to say something about this kind of problem ?

FATTU : That is one of the weaknesses, I would say. We have not reached the stage where we can define that series of problems that are precisely demanding a solution. We have many, many problems, depending upon the observer and the individual doing the talking, that are of this character. In other words, it's a subjective sort of classification rather than a professional group sort.

These problems would be classified into the kinds I have indicated here—the operational kinds. You have to put up a new school building. In order to put the scdool building you need to introduce many, many considerations. Where is land avaitable, what is the group or area this is supposed to serve, how large a school should you build—very practical kinds of question. The usual practice has been to call in a group of experts from a nearby university or consulting firm and just pass the buck to them. To say that we have any systematic methodology for dealing with this is to stretch the point. And there are people who say operational research takes problems of this sort. What we need to do is not to consider each little individval study by itself, but we need to consider the systematic way in which these things are done, considering what they are supposed to do, how do you define the questions that you are supposed to attack, and so on. But you notice this is very general and very vague and it depends on the person's interest.

One man will say, learning studies are primary, so I'm going to devote my life to doing learning studies and I intend to exclude from my focus of interest everything that does not deal with learning and learning of a very specific kind. And he devotes his energy to that. But we are in the stage where we have individual interests, each individual picking out a facet and not being too concerned with what other people are doing in that area. I don't know if this gets at the question you had in mind or not. We are not at the stage where we can say, here is the problem of learning, as I think Lee Cronbach mentions in *Text Materials in Modern Education,* where he points out that we have many studies to show that the textbook is useful in instruction; then we have a study that shows that motion pictures can do what a textbook did; then we have another study that shows that television can do what motion pictures did or what the textbook did. It reality the essential consideration is, how do you utilize these materials in combination so as to get at the criteria you had in minds ? We have very little work on criteria development in that particular sense.

BANGHART : In connection with the table where you list for these five institutions a central category of extension and public service, I would be interested particularly in the institution which seems to have the largest entry opposite extension and public services as to whether any or a considerable part of that involves this kind of action research, or are those just courses being given at off-campus centers ?

FATTU : No they are not just courses. I believe Institution D does substantially more of the kind of thing that you have in mind than does Institution E. Without looking at my notes – this is merely from recollection – I think Institution E's activity involves consulting services, of the kind I mentioned earlier, except that this is handled through the institution and not through individual pockets, so to speak. You see, there are two kinds of arrangements. In one of them the faculty member goes out as a private individual and gets a fee for doing the job. There are other institutions, and this one is of that category, where the school system pays the institution and the individual has a segment of his time allocated to this kind of activity.

FINDLEY : I think what we really need to ask is the distinction between the categories of public service and research as represented in that table.

FATTU : You have to accept what the individual institution gives you, and actually for Institution D I would say the amount for research probably should be decreased, but how much I can't say—I just have to accept their figures and put it down that way. That's one of the reasons that these kinds of data ought to be looked at very skeptically, but they do indicate a trend. When you see an institution where the amount spent for extension and public service is six and seven times that spent for research, I think it tells something about the institution.

CONRAD : Regarding this system of classification I think that at an institution like Harvard a great deal of research is classified, in the accounting system, as under "Instruction." What happens is that factory member (especially in the higher ranks) may be given a fairly light teaching load, and consequently spends a good deal of time in research. This research is commonly charged, however, to "Instruction" in the accounting of the institution, and not to "Research."

PIERCE : All the evidence I know indicates that there are so many different opinions about what educational research is that it is sometimes had to get agreement on whether or not a given job is a research job. Without seeking to define and narrow so as to exclude possible lines of inquiry, is it not possible and perhaps desirable at this stage to try at least to describe the characteristics of research that we call educational research ? If this is a good question, should a symposium of this sort give a little serious attention to this problem ?

FATTU : There are various ways of clarifying what we mean by educational research without trying to prescribe in a definition something that is likely to rule out important studies. Haven't people in other fields done that ? Is there so much difference of opinion in physics about what research is in physics ? Is there so much difference even in a field such as sociology ?

CHERRY : Let me add that my question about the support angle was directly related to this question. I think we see examples of adequate support being provided for research in certain fields because they have succeeded in ind cating what it is they are going to try to do through research much more clerly that we have in education. And they have made a case that can be supported.

TYLER : While we are speculating on the factors that may account for the relatively low status of educational research in terms of the fraction of the total budget spent on it and the kind of attention given to it, I should like to suggest that early unrealistic expectations are partly responsible. When I was an instructor at the University of Nebraska nearly forty years ago, there was a great interest in educational research and even in that state, which had previously spent money only on agricultural research, there was established in that university a bureau of educational research with some state support This was done with the optimistic view following World War I that educational research would give answers to pressing and immediate questions such as :

What do you do to get everyboody to read in the elementary school ?

What can you do to get every pupil to spell correctly ?

What can you do to achieve 100 per cent accuracy in arithmetic ?

Because of the success of psychological tests in selecting candidates for officer training in World War I and in the use of job analysis for building a shorts and effective curriculum for bricklayers and carpenters needed in the war effort, many people concluded that a bureau of educational research would quickly solve the immediate, practical problems of the Nebraska schools. But this was an expectation which was not warranted by the later results. The problems of education are not going to be answered in this way.

In a certain sense, agricultural researchers reached a kind of impasse when they sought to deal too directly with immediate, practical problems. Agriculture research gained new vitality, when different sorts of questions were studied. For example, consider the case of hybrid corn. That hybrid corn existed and many hybrids could be produced was known for many years. But agricultural researchers were not greatly interested in this field because they had a different model to guide their thinking. This model was : We have good corn. How can it best be raised ? They were conscious of the amount of water, the quality of seed, the physical and chemical characteristics of the soil, the use of fertilizer, the varying lengths of growing seasons, and these were the variables that were manipulated.

When they reached a point where corn production was up to above sixty bushels an acre, this was considered tops; maximum production had been reached. The men working on hybrid corn spent nearly twenty years before they could even get attention by agronomists, because they were geneticists. They were not working on immediate practical problems but on more theoretical ones. When, finally they got a hearing and corn production jumped, agricultural researchers in large numbers began to study more basic and theoretical problems in order to understand the more immediate ones.

I think we have gone through the stage in which the rank and file of educational workers believe that educational research has been oversold, and they really aren't going to get any solutions from research to important educational problems. I, too, think that we are not going to get answers if we look for specific devices. What we can expect to get through appropriate research is much better understanding of education and learning. Take reading as an example :

If one looks at reading as a process of a youngster adapting to the demands of the school situations, then anything that interferes with his effective functoning is a handicap in reading. We are not going to find a single factor in the situation any more than one would find a single factor when one says, "I' m sick". One can be sick for a hundred reasons, and you may be poor in reading for a hundred reasons. It is a waste of effort to look for a one-to-one correspondence between something that happened in the classroom and some quick device that will correct it. I think we ought to expect from research and to assess its values not in the specific answers it gives but in the increased understanding it gives those who are teaching and planning instruction and developing instructional materials. Looking back at earlier educational research we can easily recognize values of this sort. As one illustration, take the idea of individual differences :

These were not generally recognized prior to the research work of the early 1900's. Now, most people recognize that children are not all the same, that there are many differences among them, not only intellectual differences, but difference in attitudes, interests, and their range of emotional reactions. As another illustration, consider the idea of what children can learn. We not longer think of learning as just memorization. We talk of learning skills, habits, ways of thinking, and the like. These notions have become part of our common thinking because educational research has broadened our conception of what can be learned. It has helped us to get a more adequate, though more complex, view of what the job of education is. This means that educational research is giving us greater understanding, but it is also making education a more complex process instead of making it simpler, so that now instead of having the answers to our problems which we expected forty years ago we see a thousand problems that we didn's recognize forty years ago.

I think if we are going to get research recognized and provided for as a basic part of the activities of colleges and universities as well as of the schools, we need to have more realistic expectations of what research can do for us. It will not generally give us devices to solve practical problems, but it will enrich our whole understanding of a process which is much more complex than we used to think. This understanding will help us as practicing teachers and workers in education, and in the end the quality of education in this country will be incrersed far beyond our dreams in the 1920's. But it will be done in a way which was not anticipated in the twenties. To prevent discouragement and disillusionment about the value of research, people in education generally should know what to expect from it. Furthermore, research endeavors themselves should be conducted with this conception as its guiding principle.

Discussion Following Paper Presented by Herbert S. Conrad

LAMBERT : I would like to raise this question : Is there presently or will there be any attempts to communicate, especially with school people, the results of the projects going on under the Cooperative Research Program ? If some attempt is now being made to communicate, how effective is that effort ?

CONRAD : Public Law 531 made no provision for communication and application 'per se'. The steps that are being taken at the pesent time or have previously been taken are :

(1) an announcement of the work in 'School Life, ;

(2) the deposit of perhaps a hundred copies in various libraries ;

(3) the publication of papers. This seems to be reasonably effective so far as communicating with scholars is concerned. However, I do not see that it accomplishes effective communication with the operating staffs of the schools and with the administrative heads, with the superintendents, with the principals, with the teochers. I don't know how much money—administrative funds —could be used for that purpose under the law. Of course, the Office of Education has authority in its

regular functions to carry on the work of dissemination, but it is work that takes money and time, and what is being done strikes me personally as being inadequate. If the research is good research, it ought to be communicated.

LAMBERT : I think I agree entirely with that point of view. There are so many interesting things going on now that educators know absolutely nothing about. For instance, there is a project going on now at the University of Pittsburgh which should be of tremendous interest throughrit the rank and file in education and yet very few people even know the thing is underway. I had to go to an AERA meeting with a group of experts to get any information on the project. Now, here again I don't read 'School Life' as well as I should—I don't read a lot of things I should, for that matter—and these things drift through to me very slowly. I don't know what would be the situation, say, at the University of Kentucky or some other place.

CONRAD : I would say the Public Law 531 was not properly conceived in several respects. Two that I would like to mention are : first, the failure to recognize that a main difficulty or shortcoming of research in the past has been the failure to bridge the gap between the research information held by the scholars and the educational procedures controlled by the operating staff. Now I don't mean to imply that the researchers should become operating staffs. or that the operating staffs should become research. The way to achieve this kind of communication, ideally, it to get the operating staffs or their representatives into the research development process at the very beginning ; this is typically done in ideal "action research."

In other words, you don't start the project until you have begun communicating 'from the very beginning'. This might madify the research ; and it would certainly have some effect upon the people who could use the research. Now, all of this is more easily said than done, because operating staffs have their time pretty well taken up, and if they do take time to participate, they may be obstructive to the research rather than accessory or helpful. But the gains from helpful participation are so important that the undertaking of serious, large-scale research without operating-level cooperation should become unthinkable.

FINDLEY : This so-called University of Pittsburgh or Flanagan "Project TALENT" next year is going to involve the administration of ten hours of test or questionnaire materials in each of the eleven hundred high schools that are chosen. Either two full days or four half-days of time will be needed for this. It seems to me absolutely essential that all the forces of prestige in the world get behind this project in order to obtain the kind of cooperation that will be necessary in the many schools in which it will have to be done. I have just had a little sampling of the problem in trying to get some pilot work done rather late in the year. I may succeed, but it takes a bit of doing. I have had to start from scratch with each man I have spoken to on the whole project.

LAMBERT : The only thing I have seen on this project is a sixty-page highly technical document which would take a person two full days to read and which requires very careful study. On a project of this importance and scope, we need something written in easy-to-understandand terms. This thing is so important that practically everybody in the colleges and universities, the state departments, and so on ought to know about it. (In the 'New York Times' it occupied a column.)

CONRAD : We have been asked whether HEW is continuing to summarize completed work in 'School Life', and the answer is no. There were too many projects being completed, and it took some rather skilled writing to, shall I say, reduce it or transform it into shape for 'School Life'. There wasn't any staff to do it. This is a serious problem and I' m sure it was not envisaged in Public law 531: (I think you're right in remarking that the orignal planning failed to provide sufficient funds for the announcement of important projects, communicating the results of studies, etc).

LAMBERT : I think I would agree completely on the Point that many times we can describe what we are talking about much more effectively with a graphic portrayal of some type than we can with words. I thinks that's one of the fields of research reporting that has been greatly neglected. I don't know where it should be taught, or how it should be handled, but I do not think we are doing a very good job of it in our research courses at the graduate level or in our statistics courses.

FINDLEY : From a historical point of view, it is interesting to note that when I studied statistics as an undergraduate, from a book by Chaddock called 'Principles and Methods of Statistics,' and later, when I taught some at an undergraduate level from a book on statistical methods by Mills, there was in the back of each of these books an appendix which consisted of a report of a committee on the rules of correct and proper presentation. That was a part of instruction as I took it, but I haven't seen it since.

LAMBERT : There are several good books on graphic portrayals—four or five excellent ones have come our in the last years. But may point was not so much the accurate interpretation of statistics through graphics of various types, but rather the creative ability, the insight it takes to translate figures into some pattern that will transmit meaning directly by visual presentation. This is a big job. Some of the national magazines have developed excellent work. It costs a lot of money, but it is something we need.

Discussion Following Paper Presented by Warren Findley

PIERCE : I would like to mention something referred to regarding the limits and contributions research. If you don't mind, would you please elaborate on this a little from the point of view of limitations in the types of studies or the problems studied—limitations in methodology. I wonder if we could get some discussion on that sort of thing in the whole group at this point, now that we have had these fine papers.

FINDLEY : I react in this way, particularly in terms of the McAndrew study (of continuous promotion), for example. Now, I would say that to have concluded from this study that it is generally better to promote than to retain, for example, was altogether too simple and too sweeping a conclusion. For one thing, the study didn't show what it would mean to promote an individual repeatedly without regard to past achievement, and it completely ignored any effect such a policy might have on others in the group. Now, one might say that there is wide variation in classroom groups anyway, and that this didn't increase the variation a great deal. I would say that this variation is tremendously wide at the present time in typical school systems and even in individual schools. Some notion of the impact of that variation and what might be done about it in the way of adaptation to individual differences should, to my mind, have been an integral part of the research design.

TYLER : Doesn't this suggest a thing we were talking about this morning, that parents are involved here and their attitudes toward the schools' promotional policy are very important ? Also the attitudes of the children who are not to be promoted or something like that, are involved too—their acceptance of a new way of looking at their neighbors and the like. Isn't what you are talking about, research on almost a community-wide scale ?

FINDLEY : Yes, I would accept that as a proper extension of the thought. In some ways, though, we should also criticize, on the grounds that they were not investigating the impact on the families of the ones retared, the persons who kept on operating the schools with a rigid policy of retardation. We should criticize them just as much as we would the ones who, let's say, carelessly and too sweepingly applied a finding like this about regular promotion. I think we need to adopt the point of view that a school is a place where you educate children and that in order to educate them better you put them in certain classrooms. You do this with a view to improving their education, rather than merely having them mount a smooth and simple ladder from the first grade upward. We do have rather rare adaptations like the primary school at the present time in which the first three elementary grades are put together and then individuals are allowed to take two, three, or four years to go through that particular phase. I would say that this represents an adaptation and something which in general involves an understanding of it as a way of meeting the problem of promotions in grade organized schools.

PIERCE : Is your problem one of trying to identify some of the weaknesses of current research that does not take into account the practical situation ? I'm not clear that I understand precisely what you mean.

FINDLEY : Yes, that's a part of the problem.

TYLER : I would like to comment of on one matter that is raised by this discussion. And that is that if our efforts are going to be directed to saying only this kind of research or any given kind of research is a great thing, I would like to argue the other way around: that one of the needs is having a wider variety of research. By way of illustration, the notion of "one variable' research with all other variables eliminated is a very limiting no' tion, if it's to be the sole kind of educational research. For one-reason. I think that most of the factors we deal with in education are so inter-related that when you control one—for example, take the classic studies at Minnesota thirty years ago on class size—that when you control the size of the class and then say that everyting must go on the same except in class size you are also controlling a number of factor that are related, that are involved in class size.

There are some thing you can't do with 150 youngsters that you can do with thirty. And if you say the teaching is to be the same and the only difference is going to be that in one case 149 other kids are sitting there in class and the other case there are only twenty-nine others, this is too limiting a factor. You can't really control that variable without controlling so many other variables that the notion that it's size that does this or doesn't do it gives you some wrong impressions.

On the othe hand, there are times when a carefully controlled study, in which perhaps only one major factor is permitted to vary, may be appropriate. At the other extreme, there are times when we need studies that are largely descriptive, almost like the natural history studies of biologists. For example during the 1930's many educators became deeply concerned with the competitve spirit shown by children or their parents when a parent would boast: "My Mary got 98 and your Sally only got 96." These educators assumed that all competition of this sort was a bad thing. But natural history studies of children growing up in America suggested that the desire to excel is a common motive and often leads to socially directed efforts. In fact, many child development people began to expand the areas in which children could excel. If the desire for excelling others is well-nigh universal, and you eliminate competition in classroom activities, then you increase in the minds of youngsters the importance of something else where they can achieve status. It may be athletics, it may be the hot-rod business, it may be social activities. So as educators began to wonder why kids paid less attention to school, the natural history study of children suggested that youngsters were looking for other arenas in which they could excel when school provided limited opportunities.

These studies, although only observational ones and not controlled experiments, suggest that schools which do not inform Johnny that he is doing better than Mary may be eliminating a positive incentive for school work and stimulating him to give attention to non-school activities where he can achieve recognition.

I'm just trying to suggest that we are dealing with no simple situation in educational research. Schools are concerned not only with education but also with children who are growing up, and with teachers who have their own interests, habits, problems, etc. Most of our problems need to be examined from several points of view. I do not recommend the elimination of certain kinds of studies but rather the inclusion of a wider range.

FINDLEY : I don't believe I should defend myself by saying I purposely overstated my position. I didn't carelessly overstate it. My view would be that, if we are going to make generalizations from these very carefully controlled studies, we should take into account their generalizability. McAndrew's study illustrates the failure to see the complexity of the situation in which there is not only the question of what happens to the youngster who is promoted, but what kind of a climate is poduced in the classroom - the attitude of the teacher, the attitude toward other children, the attitude of parents. And it become in some cases so complex that the problem becomes how to make variables more manageable. Wh have places for controls or for further analysis, but what we really need is to recognize the whole range of studies that have to be supported before we can really begin to get an adequate enaugh understanding of what is going on to reach proper conclusions about what needs to be done.

JOHNSON : Well, there are two aspects of the problem. How widely can one generalize from experimental data ? That's essentially the problem you have raised, of course. It exists in every field of experimental science. I think we can profitabl consider two aspects of this problem. One could be spok f as *population* generalizability and the other as *situation* generalizability. Both of them have been brought up here. One problem usually thought of in connection with generalizability is populational. The means, of course, how widely can you generalize from your experimental subjects to the population from which they have come. But the other is situational.

Now, of course, there has been a great deal of development, all of which was not reflected in the discussion. This concept of experimental design which is still taught in the schools, that we must control all conditions except the one whose effect we wish to estimate, is a totally outmoded concept of modern design. It dates back to the time of Galileo, 350 years ago. It required R. A. Fisher to come alsong to show that that model was totally inappropriate for types of problems we meet in the sciences in which the experimental material is essentially variable. This is quite in contrast with the materials we meet in physics. Modern design experiments include a single one. As Fisher stated, if you bring a single question to nature, she is incapable of giving any type of an answer. If you come to her with a well-constructed questionnaire, she may give you an answer. A very good example of that was given last Thursday at our statistical seminar [at the University of Minnesota]. We had, at that time, a well-known statistician who was presenting a topic, namely the design of experiments in the physical sciences. And the audience was largely made up of engineering students.

Now, they had been brougut up on this doctrinaire theory, namely, that we can only measure effect when we can control all the other factors. But he showed without too much difficulty and to the suprise of the people in attendance that with modern design we are capable of introducing any number of factors. He developed a factorial design there in which fifteen different factors were operating simultaneously. The effect could be measured for each of these, not only singly but in all the possible combinations, and the interaction of these factors could be assessed.

There is nothing much more complex than a school situation. We see, as a result, the operation of a very large number of factors. I think that as long as we follow the doctrinaire theory that in order to experiment we must repropuce this Galilean model we aren't going to get far. But that is long since past, in the minds of modern designers of experiments. I have a number of them under way. I wait until I think I can convince the skeptic as to how we can broaden the scope of an experiment and hence broaden what I would call the generalizability of our experimental aims, particularly from the standpoint of a situation.

If a situation is limited to a single factor, then no matter how broadly one could generalize to the population, one could not generalize beyond a single factor situation. I think education would profit greatly if there would be more people who would give serious attention to these enormous possibilities that have been developed within the last twenty-five years. Or, for example, in the whole area of what we call response surface, where we have a series of experiments. We speak of them as sequential experimentation. We start out with a simple preliminary experiment. It gives information which we utilize in our next step. We can also anticipate, on the basis of this preliminary information, what lines of attack are most profitable to pursue. You raised quite a number of questions in there, but I was not quite sure if you assumed that no attempt had been made to answer them.

FINDLEY : Let me respond to this notion of the R.A. Fisher approaches doing something to take into account more varibles than was possible under the old Pearsonian approach. I would feel that the improvement achieved by that, with respect to the extent of the total complexity, is relatively small. It becomes necessary to have other variables of somewhat the same sort and usually quantified. But the total complexity which is the school system and what reaction the parents will make and how it will affect the children over a large number of grades and so on gets to be such a large complexity that while I hail this refinement and, if I had more time, would like to say more in favour of analysis of covariance, for example, as a way of achieving statistical control without going into a matched approach, still, wouldn't you say that the improvement—may be this is not fair—is in degree ? These refinements the Fisher has done do not accomplish the improvement that would be necessary to comprehend a very large complex.

JOHNSON : Factorial desgin is an attempt to reproduce in an experimental situation a few conditions where recommendations will be made. For that reason it has very grea promise, because the greater number of important factors yo can include in experimental situations the more likely you are to approach field conditions. So it is really an attempt to mak the experiment realistic, at least in the preliminary stages. W aren't so concerned to reduce a complex into all of its elements,

We are interested in evaluating the effects and results of a large number of factors operating simultaneously. But the important safeguard in all these factors you have mentioned is provided by the only unique principle that was introduced by Fisher, namely the principle of randomization, which has apparently been overlooked.

CONRAD : Don't you need a lot of cases ?

JOHNSON : No.

CONRAD : About fifteen variables ?

JOHNSON : No. It does mean, of course, your difference would have to be larger to be detected. But so for as the validity is concerned, it is equally valid for small as large. A sample of two can be just as random as one of a thousand.

CONRAD : Would you like to bet on a sample of two ?

NAGEL : I wasn't quite sure from the early part of your paper—and in the discussion I thought perhaps you were going one way and then sometimes the other way—whether your criticisms were of controlled experiments in general or whether your criticisms were directed against a very simple sort of controlled situation. And then you quoted Lawrence Frank, I take it with approval, in his attack on analytical method, and that is something that I quite frankly don't understand. If you attack the analytical method, what do you to repalce it ? And if you attack controlled experiments in general, what do you have to replace them with ? I can understand a criticism of an oversimplified moton where you can have just one variable changing and all the other constant. I think that's certainly inadequate. But an all-out rejection of this seems to me to be throwing out the baby with the dirty water.

FINDLEY : Certainly, I think the greatest exception could be taken to the oversimplified study. Beyond that, I would say the overreliance of the inter-relations among factors without regard to their impact on the larger whole would be my concern in what I would call educational research. Now, I would not want to impede research in the behavioral sciences such as Dr. Tyler is going to talk about tomorrow morning. I would say that there are those experiments in the behavioral sciences whose results can be applied in educational research. But, to my mind, the essence of educational research is that it indicates how you can operate within a school situation, rather than a genralizability which has a fine scientific quality, but still leaves what I would call the major part of the experiment to be performed, namely application on a large scale.

NAGEL : If I may press that point. If you were to take either of these cases that you cited—either the policy of promoting or the policy of classroom size—and you consider this as an experiment carried on in the school population in a given city, in what way would the general principles of method appear ? One would criticize the isolated experiment because it is not carried on under the circumstances under which the education process normally proceeds. But in this living situaiion don't you have to make discriminations and say, "Well, *this* in some ways is responsible for *that*," and how do you do that ?

FINDLEY : You have to identify what you are looking for, or variables. The studies of class size that you mentioned were not sensitive to those variable because the identification of other relevant variables was not as well done as it is at the present time. Research workers in the behavioral sciences and social psychology, for example, have identified many of the variables that we can now consider.

Within the actual (so-called practical) complexity in which you operate, you would want to isolate for particular study certain relationships, and these you might want to study through analytical procedures. I would say that the notion of the very narrowly restricted study, though, would be less than desirable as the model to hold before the student of education as the way in which he is going to make his contribution in a school system. I think we have some tendency to reject the insistence of school people on experience in a person. There are some people, I've heard our superintendent say, who have not had thirty years' experience, they have had simply one year's experience thirty times. But there is a certain sense in which experience with operation of schools as a reality is valuable, experience a person who comes fresh from the training institution does not have.

Now, my hope would be that in training him you would teach him that this little experiment that he is learning how to do certainly involves techniques that people will want to call upon him to use at times in studying major operations. But the problems in research are defined by the situation, and you bring your techniques to bear only on certain ones of the problems to which they apply the best. They may not give you the most decisive evidence in a particular problem that you face.

NAGEL : To pursue the question further, are you saying that experience in that case may make you conscious of a number of relevant factors or variables that the so-called simple-minded experiment might not make you conscious of, and also of some of the values you seek, some of the outcomes in learning that are beyond those that he has been previously measuring ? If you take this matter of annual promotion, would you rather take two schools, each of which draws from a rather similar kind of background, has the youngsters of about the same ability and aspirations and the like, and try annual promotions no one and on the other determine promotions on the basis of achievement ? And then over a period of years assess in more adequate terms the results of that ? But you would still use this method that we think of as controlling some factors and varying others—isn't that your point ?

FINDLEY : You might do those things, but I think in some cases that kind of set-up of an experiment would be impractical. What would happen would be that the experimenters would try a new way for a certain length of time and see how it went—a very inelegant statement from a research point of view, but in practice it is probably the logical way to proceed.

It they tried it and saw how it went, they would in effect be comparing it with previous experience. There are some ways in which the logical method is still the method of controlled comparison.

It would be a controlled comparison, but not a controlled statistical comparison between two situations in which every other variable was restricted in order to see that one variable or set of variables have their effect on a total. The final judgment will be made up of a number of conclusions. I listed in respect to the television experiment all the different kinds of questions that would have to be answered, and a number of those could not be answered quantitatively. Oh, you could do some opinion polling here and there to help you in arriving at some of the decisions, but when you got through you would not be able to put together a statistical composite of the total process, and out of it produce the conclusion that more findings were in favor of this than in favor of that. You have the problem of bringing all of these rather different kinds of considerations to bear in your final solution. Every once in a while you come against one that is so stubborn as not to yield and your other arguments, however good, your other differences, however notable, do not carry the day.

NAGEL : I think what we are concerned with is that you are not throwing out the notion of analysis as itself being a useful, intellectual tool.

FINDLEY : No.

NAGEL : If you would finally come to the conclusion that we are going to continue television the way we have because we like it, and on the whole, you say, a lot of factors we thought make it good, this is not as useful knowledge, as well as not as good in other intellectual terms, as though you are able to identify and come to more analytic conclusions.

FINDLEY : *Those* things, we found, were accomplished in television, although we sacrificed *these*.

NAGEL : You have some kind of analysis and comparison. That sntellectual activity is still going on.

FINDLEY : Yes, I would say that is going on and I would perhaps agree. What you are forcing me to say is correct. I would not repudiate the analytic procedure with respect to some elements of this whole study, but I would see these elements in relation to the total study and I would see as a concern—at least as great a concern as what we could find by some of these carefully controlled analyses—matters with which we would have to deal in terms of a judgment, because you couldn't come up with any of these quantitative comparisons.

NAGEL : You might find difficulty with quantitative comparisons, but even if they are dealt with only in some loose qualitative way, some distinction, I take it, has to be introduced. And, if I may venture a suggestion, in your quoting Lawrence Frank on this point, it is a bit of red herring. To dismiss analytic methods, it seems to me, is to surrender one's intellectual birthright, really.

JOHNSON : An illustration of what is probably being indicated grew out of what we call uniformity trial data in agriculture. There are two sets of figures that we ordinarily use in trying to give any meaning to this, where the same treatment was given to a number of subdivisions of an acre of land, making all the conditions but one as nearly uniform as possible. There are two sources of variation, or two sources that give rise to variation, and they must be taken into account in experimental work. Otherwise, you see, you are really crediting it to a false origin. This change in material that takes place you are ascribing to the factors that you introduced, and that must be safeguarded. The one source is the intrinsic variation in the material itself, in all biological, psychological material. The intrinsic variability is one source of a significant property.

The other sources of variation is the total impossibility of being able to replicate completely the techniques of the experiment itself. The only way of isolating out this sort of a variation from what we would call the real effect is by a safeguard secured by the principle of randomization. But when this has been done then it is possible to isolate out this source. If it is not done, the variation is included in what we call experimental errors and thus makes this error larger than it should be and the error component is confounded with the other sources of the variation. So the variation must be clearly indicated, and the control over it must make that necessary. Otherwise, there could be no confidence in the conclusions that you draw. Even in a field such as astronomy, for example, Neyman of the University of California has been able to get the astronomers out there, at least, to recognize the great variation that occurred in repeated measurements. They had evolved the practice of taking only a single measurement, assuming that that would be all that was needed. He got them to try out measurement after measurement and they found out that no two of the results agreed exactly.

The only way of analyzing or removing that error was through statistical methods. so that was one way of convincing them to take a pretty respectable look at statistical methods. I'm almost afraid of anything that you leave entirely to your own personal observation. *These* factors can't be measured or *these* variables can't be handled in *this* way, you say, but you seem to infer that you yourself by your impressions are able to evaluate their influence.

FATTU : This is a point that bothered me : the total complexity which is the school and the impact of particular factors on the whole. We talk about the tremendous mass of data that is handled by the people who deal with weather and the people who deal with guided missiles, or with the design of a new aircraft. There are considerably more data in such cases than you find in the Altanta schools, and I suspect in the Chicago school system. And yet one can deal with these data systematically. What it seems to me is that we have failed in defining what we are trying to do. We have failed to specify the operations by which we operate and we have failed to define what we mean by data. As some of engincers indicate, without specification, information colllected is merely addom noise; it does not become data. I think we have spent a great deal of time discussing what the group last summer (this is a group of psychologists out in Colorado) called "confirmatory activities." We have spent very little time discussing what we call the creative activities, those associated with the first phase of inquiry, with deciding how we define a problem in the problem area.

How do we establish the kind of complexities, if you please, that we are to investigate ? Now, if we study data processing methods in business, if we study the efforts of the operations research people, if we study the methods used by engineers and weathermen in analyzing data, we can see the ways of handling millions and millions of items of data very effectively. But even these people don't have anything of help to us in theory development, that is in identifying what we shall call data and what we shall not call data. I am not convinced that the somewhat casual kind in this action research is the answer.

FINDLEY : Let's respond to several of these remarks. If I were addressing a group of school administrators on the subject of the importance of educationl research, I would probably be outlining the opposite face of the coin with respect to the importance of making as explicit as possible those policies that could be adopted to bring into experimental comparison matters on which they were going to make their decisions without recourse to systematic data. I think today I have been speaking to you as an educational administrator. Actually, I feel there is a need for all of your refined techniques to be imbedded very deeply and superficially in these larger complexities. And it is important to have that before the minds of your graduate students in education. Now, if you are teaching them in a department of psychology in the graduate school of arts and sciences you may not have to do this. But if you are teaching them educational psychology and preparing them to become psychologists who will be useful to school systems, then

I would say that this notion of organized complexities, into which any finding has to be inserted, is, I think, a crucial idea to present. Perhaps that explains my way of stating it.

FATTU : You say that one of our major difficulties is not one of how to handle data, but rather deciding what we want the data for ?

NAGEL : Yes, and what are the data we want. And we become sensitive to data as we develop the kind of more carefully controlled studies that have been done by the behavioral scientists. There are, I am sure, data that are of far greater significance than any we collect at the present time, but that we are not collecting simply because we are not sensitized to lhem. They are all about us, but we are not aware of them. We will not become aware of these data until we have a structure of systematic theory development stemming out of related sequences of studies similar to those of the behavioral scientists. Physical science did not make progress so long as it remained at the common sense level. Such progress finally came when systematic theory evolved out of continuing series of experimental studies. In turn, these studies suggested new studies, new data, new theory. There isn't anything in action research, which operates at a common-sense level and does not get into abstractions and theorizing, that would help you identify those kinds of things.

If I have been following this discussion, two things stand out. One is that research on any problem in education is immensely complicated because of the tremendous complexity in the array of variables. Aud them the second thing is that we do have new ways of analyzing data that can take into account these multiple factors. What we haven't said thus far, I think, is that with the new knowledge of processing data and the new knowledge of the multiplicity of inter-related factors operating in a given situation we perhaps need to go back and take a new look at how we define a problem upon which to do research.

This is where philosophers, I think, and the kinds of disciplines that they have would be of considerable help to us. And I think we haven't taken enough trouble to define abstractly. if you please—not practically what is important in these situations. For example, in these studies of class size and their effect on learning, where do you find reference made to the specific objectives of learning in the given situation that affects class size with which you are dealing ? A good deal of the research on such problems has been made on the assumption that the particular pattern of organization we now have in the school is the best one anyway, apparently because we haven't questioned that in the research at all. And I think we could go ahead and name half the other kinds of assumptions that we seem to have implicity accepted that have a great deal to do with how we can do the job of research in the first place and certainly how we are going to interpret what we find.

TYLER : In regard to the comment on the class size studies, for some reason there were about two hundred done before anyone took into explicit consideration what education is for, what were the goals of the process. The earlier studies simply assumed that any standardized tests was appropriate regardless of whether it measured the progress of students toward objectives likely to be affected by class size. Only in more recent years have these studies tested several kinds of learning outcomes to see which are related to class size.

I think there is quite a difference between research that is planned to answer an immediate practical question and the kind of research that is conducted to give better understanding of what is going on in the educational process. Studies of class size illustrate this point. Beginning in 1929, the biology departments at Ohio State got very much interested in the question of what they could do with class size, and began to carry on some investigations, including differential measures of what happened in classes of different sizes. They found, for example, that there was no difference in the amount that the students remembered of textbook material in classes of different sizes. They even carried the study to a group of sdentswhotn did not attend class at all but simply studied by themselves for the examinations. This group also remembered textbook material as well as those in classes. But, they were not content to test only for recall, they tested for the ability to analyze biological problems and to figure out what kind of experiments might be carried on. On these objectives students in small classes made somewhat greater progress than those in large classes.

However, the point I particularly wished to make is that, as this series of experiments went on over about five or six years, the chief value obtained was new understanding on the part of the teaching staff. During the first year when they found that in several respects the large classes were doing as well as the small ones, they began to say, "Well, now look, if we are not getting any better results than in the large classes, why not ? What could we do ?" They began to devise ways to reorganize their small classes to do a better job. And the next year students in the small classes did do better. This led the teacher to say, "Now look, what can we do to improve our large classes ?" Now it's one thing where research is trying to give you more and more understanding of a process that teachers and others can control, and it's another thing where you are assuming that teachers' attitudes, insights, and procedures are more or less fixed. My plea is not to conduct only research where no answers can be obtained but rather we ought to remember that both are important in education. We've got some immediate administrative problems which we will have to decide the best we can, and in some cases it will be on rather gross data. But we've got the continuing problem of understanding this total process of learning such matters as, what students are thinking about, what guides them and stimulates them, what is on the minds of teachers, what guides and stimulates them. And this is a never-ending process. We ought to get more and more information. And certainly we are going to use a good deal of analytical method in this connection, but also we shall be putting things together as we generalize and as we use what knowledge we obtain.

FATTU : I think several different kinds of research need to go on. To my mind, what you are proposing there, feeding back to two different groups the results of their success with students, would not in any way be out of place in an organized complexity. It seems to me that this is a perfectly legitimate operational study. One of the notions that we challenged by other conferees was that certain factors have to be studied in the great variety of their ramifications throughout the whole system, not by themselves. Now, there are certain factors that can be made to operate within a limited field and one can properly say that one need have no concern about their ramifying out into some other part of the system, because the effects can only be judged good or bad within the limited situation in which they are applied, and there is room for a kind of straightforward comparative approach. I still like the nation of trying to imbed whatever findings we have in a reality that is not to be found exclusively in the studies in which important factors are controlled. I would say the factors that need to be taken into account in many cases are of a different order of magnitude, in a different zone of operation, than the factors that are taken account of admittedly very finely and better by the newer advances in statistical method.

That's not a statistical problems, that's a problem for the investigator. We can't tell him how to handle it. What these new factors are, that's what the psychologist does. We can help in identifying what these new factors are. That's the problem of the investigator.

In other words, our statistical methods of handling several variables don't help us much if the investigator doesn't even recognize this variable. And that's what frequently happens.

JOHNSON : At a little higher level, the problem, as I see it here, is encountered in a different way in what we call, sometimes, a statistical decision function as compared to the problem of statistical inferences. Some say that all problems can be subsumed under the statistical decisions function. I don't think they can. But in the use of the statistical decisions function the assumption is that we are finding out these results in order to take action of some kind. At the level of inference, since isn't necessarily interested only in finding out those things that lead you to make a decision and put you in action. It is also interested in adding to our scientific knowledge.

don't think they can. But in the use of the statistical decisions function the assumption is that we are finding out these results in order to take action of some kind. At the level of inference, since isn't necessarily interested only in finding out those things that lead you to make a decision and put you in action. It is also interested in adding to our scientific knowledge.

Bibliography

General

Schluter, W.C. *How to do Research Work.* New York : Prentice-Hall, Inc., 1927.

Ogg, F.A. *Research in the Humanistic and Social Sciences.* New York : The Century Co., 1928.

Gee, Wilson, Edited with introduction by. *Research in the Social Sciences.* New York : The Macmillan Co., 1929.

Educational Research

Buckingham, B.R. *Research for Teachers.* New York ; Silver, Burdett & Co., 1926.

Kelley, Truman L. *Scientific Method* : Its Function in Research and in Education. Columbus : The Ohio State University Press, 1929.

Waples, Douglas, and Tyler, R.W. *Research Methods and Teachers' Problems.* New York : The Macmillan Co., 1930.

Technique

Crawford, C.C. *The Technique of Research in Education.* Los Angeles, California : University of Southern California, 1928.

Good, C.V. *How to do Research in Education.* Baltimore : Warwick and York, Inc., 1928.

Bixler, H,H. *Check Lists for Educational Research.* New York : Bureau of Publications, Teachers College, Columbia University, 1928.

Monroe, W.S., and Engelhart, M.D. *The Techniques of Educational Research.* Urbana : University of Illinois Bulletin, XXV, No. 18 (10th January, 1928) ; Educational Research Bulletin No. 38.

Whitney, Frederick Lamson. *Methods in Educational Research.* New York : D. Appleton and Co., 1931.

Barr, A.S.. and Rudisill, Mabel. *An Annotated Bibliography on the Methodology of Scientific Research as Applied to Education.* Madison, Wisconsin : University of Wisconsin, Bureau of Educational Research Bulletin, No. 13, 1931.

Results

Monroe, W.S. *Ten Years of Educational Research,* 1918–1927. Urbana : University of Illinois Bulletin, XXV, No. 51 (21st August, 1928) ; Educational Research Bulletin No. 42.

Good, C.V., Collins, W.L., and Gregory, C.A., Compiled by. *Graduate Thesis in Education,* 1927—1931. Abstracts, I. Cincinnati, Ohio : Teachers College, University of Cincinnati, 1931.

Peters, C.C., and Struck, F.T. *Abstracts of Studies in Education at the Pennsylvania State College.* Penn State Studies in Education, No. 2. Pennsylvania : School of Education, Pennsylvania State College, 1931.

Alexander, C , and others. *Educational Research* : Suggestions and Sources of Data with Specific Reference of Administration. 3rd edition, revised and enlarged. New York : Bureau of Publications, Teachers College, Columbia University, 1931.

U.S Department of the Interior. ***Bibliography of Research Studies in Education***, 1929—1930. Prepared in the Library Division by Edith A. Wright. Washington : Superintendent of Documents, 1931.

Organisation and Administration

Chapman, H.B. *Organised Research in Education.* Ohio State University Studies. Bureau of Educational Research Monographs, No. 7. Columbus : The Ohio State University Press, 1927.

Wright, E.A. *Organisation and Functions of Research Bureau in City School Systems.* U.S. Office of Education Leaflet No. 2. Washington : Superintendent of Documents, 1931.

